THE FLETCHER JONES FOUNDATION

HUMANITIES IMPRINT

The Fletcher Jones Foundation has endowed this imprint to foster innovative and enduring scholarship in the humanities.

The publisher gratefully acknowledges the generous support of the Fletcher Jones Foundation Humanities Endowment Fund of the University of California Press Foundation.

JUMPING FROGS

UNDISCOVERED, REDISCOVERED, AND CELEBRATED

WRITINGS OF MARK TWAIN

Named after one of Mark Twain's best-known and beloved short stories, the Jumping Frogs series of books brings neglected treasures from Mark Twain's pen to readers.

1. *Is He Dead? A Comedy in Three Acts,* by Mark Twain. Edited with foreword, afterword, and notes by Shelley Fisher Fishkin. Text established by the Mark Twain Project, The Bancroft Library. Illustrations by Barry Moser.

2. *Mark Twain's Helpful Hints for Good Living: A Handbook for the Damned Human Race,* by Mark Twain. Edited by Lin Salamo, Victor Fischer, and Michael B. Frank of the Mark Twain Project, The Bancroft Library.

3. *Mark Twain's Book of Animals,* by Mark Twain. Edited with introduction, afterword, and notes by Shelley Fisher Fishkin. Texts established by the Mark Twain Project, The Bancroft Library. Illustrations by Barry Moser.

4. *Dear Mark Twain: Letters from His Readers.* Edited by R. Kent Rasmussen.

5. *A Family Sketch and Other Private Writings,* by Mark Twain, Livy Clemens, and Susy Clemens. Edited by Benjamin Griffin of the Mark Twain Project, The Bancroft Library.

A FAMILY SKETCH

AND

OTHER PRIVATE WRITINGS

A Family Sketch
and
Other Private Writings

~

BY

Mark Twain

Livy Clemens

Susy Clemens

EDITED BY

Benjamin Griffin

OF THE MARK TWAIN PROJECT

UNIVERSITY OF CALIFORNIA PRESS

University of California Press, one of the most distinguished university presses in the United States, enriches lives around the world by advancing scholarship in the humanities, social sciences, and natural sciences. Its activities are supported by the UC Press Foundation and by philanthropic contributions from individuals and institutions. For more information, visit www.ucpress.edu.

University of California Press
Oakland, California

Library of Congress Cataloging-in-Publication Data

Twain, Mark, 1835–1910.
　[Works. Selections]
　A family sketch and other private writings / Mark Twain, Livy Clemens, Susy Clemens ;
edited by Benjamin Griffin of the Mark Twain Project.
　　　pages cm. — (Jumping frogs: undiscovered, rediscovered, and celebrated writings of Mark Twain ; 5)
　Includes bibliographical references.
　ISBN 978-0-520-28073-1 (hardback) — ISBN 978-0-520-95963-7 (ebook)
　　1. Twain, Mark, 1835–1910—Family.　2. Authors, American—19th century—Biography.　I. Clemens,
Olivia Langdon, 1845–1904.　II. Clemens, Susy, 1872–1896.　III. Griffin, Benjamin,
1968–　editor.　IV. Title.
　　PS1302.G75　2014
　　818'.409--dc23　　　　　　　　　　　　　　　　　　　　　　　　　2014008634
　　[B]

Manufactured in the United States of America

23　22　21　20　19　18　17　16　15　14
10　9　8　7　6　5　4　3　2　1

The paper used in this publication meets the minimum requirements of ANSI/NISO z39.48–1992 (R 2002) (*Permanence of Paper*).

CONTENTS

INTRODUCTION

This book publishes in full, for the first time, the two most revealing of Mark Twain's private writings about his family life, neither of them actually written for publication. In their company we have placed closely related writing by his wife, Olivia ("Livy"), and by his eldest daughter, Susy. In this collection the reader will find Samuel Langhorne Clemens in the context of the daily life he shared with Livy, their three daughters, a great many servants, and an imposing array of pets.

~~~

The exuberant "Family Sketch" has its origins in Mark Twain's response to unimaginable loss. Susy Clemens died on 18 August 1896, at the age of twenty-four, succumbing to meningitis in the Hartford, Connecticut, house where she and her sisters were raised. Her father, mother, and sister Clara were in England, having just completed a tour around the world. Alerted by cablegram to her illness, mother and daughter crossed the Atlantic to be with Susy. She died before they arrived. Starting in these first days of his grief, and continuing at intervals over the next five years, Mark Twain tried to write a memorial to Susy, accumulating a large mass of mostly unfinished manuscript. Some of this material was eventually incorporated into his *Autobiography,* which he dictated and compiled in 1906–9; but most of it remains unpublished. Inevitably, his project of a memorial to Susy was never completed. Years later, his secretary, Isabel V. Lyon, recorded his admission that he "was never able to write a memorial of her. It was never anything but a Lament, & couldn't ever be anything but that."[1]

Yet from these abandoned papers, full of loose ends and repetitions, there arose one complete and startling essay. It springs from the same impetus as the rest of the "Susy memorial" manuscripts: its original title was "In Memory of Olivia Susan Clemens, 1872–1896." But having set out to commemorate Susy, Clemens found "A Family Sketch" growing under his hands to become an account of the entire household—family and servants too. Servants especially, we might say; for herein will be found his fullest and most revealing account of the household servants, their characters and their part in the Clemenses' lives. Four of them, especially long-serving, are singled out for greater attention: Patrick McAleer (coachman), George Griffin (butler), Katy Leary (lady's maid; housekeeper, after Livy's death), and Rosina Hay (nursemaid). To these must be added the remarkable account of Maria McLaughlin, wet-nurse, of brief tenure and immortal fame. Free from the anguished note that runs through the other Susy manuscripts, "A Family Sketch" describes the Clemens family in the period of its flourishing.

The manuscript was not composed at a single sitting. From physical evidence and mentions of dates, we can judge it was mainly composed in 1901–2; yet parts of it incorporate or revise pages clearly written nearer the date of Susy's death. Clemens returned to the manuscript around 1906 and made a few revisions. If he was thinking of using this material in the *Autobiography*, he decided against it. His plans for the sketch remain unknown. A reference in the sketch itself to the personal friends "to whom this small book will go" was later deleted by the author. It is not even certain what happened to this manuscript when Clemens died in 1910. It was not part of the Mark Twain Papers bequeathed by Clara, his sole heir, to the University of California in 1949. Perhaps at that time it was already in the Doheny Library in southern California, or that library may have acquired it in one of several sales of Clara's property in the 1950s. Sold when the Doheny collection was broken up in 1988, the manuscript passed to the James S. Copley Library in San Diego; that library was sold at auction in 2010, and "A Family Sketch" was acquired by The Bancroft Library. It is now in the Mark Twain Papers; this is its first complete publication.

The last "character" drawn in "A Family Sketch" is that of Mary Ann Cord, the cook at Sue Crane's farm outside Elmira, New York, where the Clemenses spent the summers. Clemens, for whom endings were always a problem, requires his editor to conclude the "Sketch" by appending the lightly fictionalized account of "Aunty Cord" which he had published in the *Atlantic Monthly* in 1874: "A True Story, Repeated Word for Word as I Heard It." This short tale has, as Clemens warned *Atlantic* editor William Dean Howells, "no humor in it."[2] Aunt Rachel (Cord's fictional incarnation) is introduced as a laughing, loyal servant—uncomfortably resembling, at first glance, the "happy darky" of antebellum nostalgia. When "Mr. C." asks her how it happens that she has reached the age of sixty and "never had any trouble," Rachel's aspect changes, and she unfolds her own story of slavery, the forced dispersion of her family, and its (partial) restoration. Mark Twain expressively deploys spatial and physical relationships between the speaker and the listeners: Rachel starts out "sitting respectfully below our level, on the steps" of the porch, but rises midway through her story, "and now she towered above us, black against the stars." As she brings her tale to its close, Rachel is even manhandling Mr. C., "pushing," "grabbing" and "shoving" his foot, clothing and hair—familiarities which, under slavery, would have been whipping or killing offenses.[3]

As his first publication in the *Atlantic Monthly*, the country's preeminent literary journal, "A True Story" was a career landmark for Mark Twain; and if the publication opened up new opportunities for him, so did the subject matter and the technique. In his future writing the use of dialect narration, and the exploration of race and slavery, would figure prominently. "A True Story" is presented here in a freshly prepared text based on the original manuscript. The spelling—obviously significant in the case of dialect narration—hews close to Mark Twain's manuscript, giving Rachel's speech a starker and simpler aspect—one that was obscured by the fussy spelling and punctuation imposed by the *Atlantic Monthly* editors in 1874 and reproduced in all subsequent reprintings.

"A Record of the Small Foolishnesses of Susie & 'Bay' Clemens (Infants)" is a manuscript record kept by the parents of the sayings and doings of their daughters. The title reflects the tally of daughters at the time the record was begun; youngest daughter Jean would not be born until 1880. The record accumulated between 1876 and 1885; three entries are in Livy's hand, the rest in her husband's. Mark Twain usually referred to it as "the Children's Record." This is its first complete publication.

In an autobiographical dictation of 5 September 1906 Mark Twain said:

> It is years since I have examined the Children's Record. I have turned over a few of its pages this morning. This book is a record in which Mrs. Clemens and I registered some of the sayings and doings of the children, in the long ago, when they were little chaps. Of course we wrote these things down at the time because they were of momentary interest—things of the passing hour, and of no permanent value—but at this distant day I find that they still possess an interest for me and also a value, because it turns out that they were registrations of character. The qualities then revealed by fitful glimpses, in childish acts and speeches, remained as a permanency in the children's characters in the drift of the years, and were always afterward clearly and definitely recognizable.[4]

On this subject, it ought to be remarked that accurate registrations of character may nevertheless be faulty registrations of fact. Take the anecdote of Clara at prayer (page 68): from a contemporary letter from Livy to her husband, we know that it was actually Susy who declared "O, one's enough!"[5] But this utterance fit Mark Twain's idea of Clara's character—worldly, pragmatic—better than it did his idea of Susy's; he was not present when the words were said; and despite Livy's accurate report, he unconsciously transferred the saying to Clara. Certainly "Small

Foolishnesses" has aims in view beyond mere accurate reporting. Longer entries, clustering mostly around 1880, attain an essayistic character, fluent and discursive.

To this long-accumulating manuscript, the brief "At the Farm" forms a kind of pendant. Written in the summer of 1884, it picks up where the earlier manuscript leaves off. It gives valuable particulars of Jean, who, as the youngest of the girls, was underrepresented in "Small Foolishnesses."

Livy's diary entries from the summer of 1885 were written in what had started out as a guest-book at the Clemenses' Hartford house. Since they persistently forgot to ask guests to sign it, Livy resolved in June 1885 to "make some use of it," keeping a diary in its pages through November of that year. (Further entries, not reproduced here, were added in 1892–93, 1894, and 1902.) Writers on Mark Twain have typically found it difficult to grasp Livy's character; the entries included here will not, perhaps, fundamentally alter this situation, but it has seemed important to let her voice be heard in the present collection. Her writing style is seldom more than functional, but there are compensations. She treats many of the same events related elsewhere in this volume from other family members' perspectives; and, even in the brief compass of this selection, it will be seen that her frame of reference is as broad as her husband's—quite as many works of science and literature are referred to in her few pages as could be found in an equivalent stretch of Mark Twain's notebooks. His own accounts of Livy's character, in these writings and elsewhere, are hyperbolic, and no easier to interpret because of that. He represents her as an untarnishable character, incapable of wrong; it follows that she is the perfect mother, from whose ruling there is no appeal. But Susy, in the biography of her father shortly to be discussed, allows herself more latitude: "Mamma's oppinions and ideas upon the subject of bringing up children has always been more or less of a joke in our family." It is indeed difficult to locate the point upon which these testimonies converge.

"Somewhere between the ages of nine and twelve Susy fell to scribbling a little in a fragmentary way," Mark Twain wrote, "but she was all of thirteen years old before she deliberately essayed authorship."[6] He was delighted, in April 1885, to find that she was composing a biography of himself: "the dearest compliment I could imagine, and the most gratifying." Just weeks after her death, he remembered that time:

> Poor fair & slender & comely little maid, with her plaited tails hanging down her back, what a brave enterprise it was! And we practised treasons against her—her mother & I—for when we found out by accident that she was at this secret labor of love we stole her book every night after she was asleep, & carried it to bed & read it. It was delicious reading, because of its naivety, its penetration, its sure touch, its curiously accurate exploration of my character, & the bland frankness of its judgments upon the questionable features of it. . . . Her studies & travels interfered with the biography; and increasingly; but she never gave up her purpose of completing it. She added a page or so to it at intervals, both at home & abroad; for it shared with Shakespeare the honorable distinction of being carried around with her wherever she went.

Susy's biography breaks off, mid-sentence, in July 1886. Mark Twain believed she had continued it into 1894, but if there were any addenda to the text, they have not been found.

Susy's work immortalizes a time when the family was flourishing and the mutual affection and admiration of father and daughter were strong. Little need be said in its explication—Mark Twain did that, inimitably, after Susy's death. His scheme for a "memorial to Susy" included publication of her book, with his comments.[7] The book did not appear, and he eventually inserted much of the biography, again with his comments, into his own *Autobiography*. When portions of the *Autobiography* ran as a serial in the *North American Review* (1906–7), passages from Susy's document figured prominently in the selections. "I cannot bring myself to change any line or word in Susy's sketch of me," Mark Twain wrote. "The spelling is frequently desperate, but it was Susy's, and it shall stand. . . . To correct it would alloy it, not refine it."[8] Actually, he did modify many of Susy's misspellings, and inserted clarifications of fact. A different approach was taken by Charles Neider in his 1985 edition. Neider intended to give Susy's orthography as she left it; his transcription, however, was careless, and he included Mark Twain's comments and diversions, as printed in his *Autobiography*. The present edition aims to preserve Susy's spelling and grammar, with minimal editorial correction, and to print her little book as she wrote it, without the intervention of her famous father.

~~~

What kind of family is sketched here?

It revolves, naturally, around Mark Twain. The subject of Susy's biography is a paragon, perfect except for his teeth; and what a moment she catches him at! Here is "papa," just turned fifty, with birthday encomia arriving from famous writers around the world; here he is, publishing the memoirs of his friend Ulysses S. Grant, and arranging a personal audience for Susy; here he is, having just published a book called *Huckleberry Finn*, and writing one called *A Connecticut Yankee in King Arthur's Court*. The family would have revolved around the father anyway, given the customs of the time; given in addition that he *is* Mark Twain, this was doubly certain.

With present good fortune comes apprehensiveness about the future, a quality not absent from Livy's 1885 diary, and expressed more complexly by Mark Twain. He does not suppress a morbid strain in his accounts of the children's dangers and narrow scrapes: the fires and dunkings and perilous heights, the near-tragedy in the Oat Bin. What are we to see in his small ghoulishnesses: the parent's relief at having escaped the worst? Or is it showmanship, the will to keep us at the edge of our seats, like the spellbound audience of "The Golden Arm"? In Mark Twain's case, can the two impulses even be distinguished?

The household religion, we gather, is essentially the religion of Livy's family—endorsed, of course, by her husband, who seems to have muted his skepticism for the children's sake. It is a liberal and nearly demythologized faith; yet God is distinctly present to the children's minds. God has ordained whatever exists, and is allowed to stay up all night. The moral and ethical character of Jesus is stressed, and prayer is believed to be efficacious; but spiritualist innovations ("the Mind Cure") are also tried. Reverence is expected of the children, yet their naïve blasphemies are secretly enjoyed by the parents, and are treasured up in the book of "Small Foolishnesses." In Susy, the intellectual prodigy, we see a growing theological sophistication. In her observation that, as the Indians "were wrong" heretofore, *we* may be wrong now, she has rediscovered in her own person the suspension of dogmatic conclusions that defines liberal theology; from which follows naturally her minimalist prayer, simply "*that there may be a God—and a heaven—*OR SOMETHING BETTER." Mark Twain watches her moral and intellectual development, fascinated.

Personal morals are strict. Corporal punishments—spanking ("the spat"), the punitive trip with the parent to "the bathroom"—are employed. Clara has a knack of enjoying her punishments; Susy's nervous intensity is already punishment enough. Lying is always wrong. ("They did not get this prejudice from me," Mark Twain comments.) The parents' campaign against the children's apparently innate mendacity is unsparing; when it finally takes effect, the girls "lean toward an almost hypercritical exactness"; a subtle revenge. The Golden Rule, attention to how the Other must feel, is consciously driven home.

The high moral tone is relieved occasionally by clowning, mostly instigated or inspired by Mark Twain. Susy enjoys and records her father's crude Western anecdotes, his homely ode to the donkey, and his parody (*she* thinks it is his) of the hymn "There is a happy land." Gentility and decency are tempered by these eruptions of frontier life, a life the girls knew and enjoyed—at second hand. The legend, for it was already that, of Mark Twain's life was a shared possession. With his raw Western youth counterpointing his respectable maturity, he seemed to straddle two worlds. Their own world, of genteel femininity, is sharply circumscribed, after the fashion of the time. Clemens was not entirely facetious when he said of his daughters: "I have carefully raised them as young ladies who don't know anything and can't do anything."[9] Being a lady excluded most gainful or useful employments; the Clemenses, progressive in many respects, were orthodox in this. But of course the girls were highly educated. With their mother and a series of tutors they studied music, history, languages (German, French, and Latin), and the sciences.

For all its value as a kind of group biography, this volume is far from complete. In the early 1890s, bad investments and business troubles drove Mark Twain to economize by moving the family to Europe; the Hartford house was shuttered, and the summers at Quarry Farm were no more. Information about the Clemenses' lives after these events is basically beyond the scope of this collection, and must be sought elsewhere. The sketches of the Clemenses in the Biographical Directory could be a jumping-off point. Neider's introduction (in *Papa*) contains information on Susy's later years. Clara published *My Father, Mark Twain* in 1931. Mark Twain chronicled his own life, private and public, in his unorthodox *Autobiography;* the Mark Twain Project is in the process of publishing a critical, annotated edition.[10]

One consequence of publishing these private and unpolished documents together is that there are repetitions or reduplications of several sayings or incidents. If the book is read straight through, Jean's theological perplexity about the ducks will be encountered three times; Rosina Hay will be identified on five separate occasions as a "German nurse"; and so forth. It has been thought better to accept these repetitions than to alter the texts; repetition is the very life of anecdote.

Brief explanations of some of the less readily grasped allusions will be found in About the Texts at the back of this volume, which also describes the manuscripts and their treatment by the editor. The Biographical Directory identifies persons, focusing on their relation to the Clemens family; it includes somewhat fuller entries on the Clemens family themselves.

The Mark Twain Project hopes that this publication will be welcome to that elusive person to whom our author is so much indebted—the general reader; and that easy access to sound texts of these manuscripts will be useful to Mark Twain specialists, literary researchers, and historians of the family.

Benjamin Griffin
Berkeley, 2014

NOTES

(Book titles abbreviated here are given in full in Works Cited.)

1. Lyon 1907, entry for 14 January.

2. Letter to William Dean Howells, 2 September 1874: *L6,* 217.

3. In his study of the manuscript of "A True Story," Makoto Nagawara notes that some of these spatial effects are the result of careful revision (Nagawara 1989).

4. *AutoMT2,* 222.

5. On 12 August 1877, Livy wrote her husband from Quarry Farm:

> This afternoon Susie and I had a rather sad time because she told me a lie—she felt very unhappy about it—This evening after her prayer I prayed that she might be forgiven for it, then I said "Susie don't you want to pray about it and ask for your self to be forgiven?" She said "Oh one is enough"— (Mark Twain Papers).

6. This quotation, and the block quotation which follows it, are from the Susy Memorial Manuscripts, Box 31a, no. 4a (Mark Twain Papers). The quotation beginning "the dearest compliment . . ." is from "Small Foolishnesses"; see page 93.

7. Clemens spoke to his secretary Isabel Lyon of doing this even after he had quoted much of Susy's book in his *Autobiography*. She wrote:

> Then after dinner when I had played the Lohengrin Wedding March 3 times while he lay curled up in a corner of the couch with his black cape wrapped about him, we talked a little about music, & then he talked about what he wants done with the parts of Susy's biography of him as it appears in the Autobiography. When he is gone he would like to have it published in book form,—Susy's biography of him & his comment upon it, for that will stand as a memorial of her (Lyon 1907, entry for 14 January).

8. *AutoMT1*, 338.

9. Clemens made this remark in a statement before the Senate and House Committees on Patents, 7 December 1906; see *AutoMT2*, 338.

10. Clara Clemens 1931. A selective list of further reading on the Clemens family might start with Albert Bigelow Paine's authorized biography of Mark Twain (*MTB*), and continue with Lawton 1925; Harnsberger 1960 and 1982; Salsbury 1965; and Jerome and Wisbey 2013. *"The Loveliest Home That Ever Was"* (Courtney 2011) is a finely illustrated book on the Clemenses' Hartford house.

~~~

MARK TWAIN

A Family Sketch

Susy was born in Elmira, New York, in the house of her grandmother, Mrs. Olivia Langdon, on the 19th of March, 1872, and after tasting and testing life and its problems and mysteries under various conditions and in various lands, was buried from that house the 20th of August, 1896, in the twenty-fifth year of her age.

She was a magazine of feelings, and they were of all kinds and of all shades of force; and she was so volatile, as a little child, that sometimes the whole battery came into play in the short compass of a day. She was full of life, full of activity, full of fire, her waking hours were a crowding and hurrying procession of enthusiasms, with each one in its turn differing from the others in origin, subject and aspect. Joy, sorrow, anger, remorse, storm, sunshine, rain, darkness—they were all there: they came in a moment, and were gone as quickly. Her approval was passionate, her disapproval the same, and both were prompt. Her affections were strong, and toward some her love was of the nature of worship. Especially was this her attitude toward her mother. In all things she was intense: in her this characteristic was not a mere glow, dispensing warmth, but a consuming fire.

Her mother was able to govern her, but any others that attempted it failed. Her mother governed her through her affections, and by the aids of tact, truthfulness barren of trick or deception, a steady and steadying firmness, and an even-handed fairness and justice which compelled the child's confidence. Susy learned in the beginning that there was one who would not say to her the thing which was not so, and whose promises, whether of reward or punishment, would be strictly kept; that there was one whom she must always obey, but whose commands would not come in a rude form or with show of temper.

As a result of this training, Susy's obediences were almost always instant and willing, seldom reluctant and half-hearted. As a rule they were automatic, through habit, and cost no noticeable effort. In the nursery—even so early—Susy and her mother became friends, comrades, intimates, confidants, and remained so to the end.

While Susy's nursery-training was safeguarding her from offending other people's dignity, it was also qualifying her to take care of her own. She was accustomed to courteous speech from her mother, but in a Record which we kept for a few years of the children's small sayings and doings I find note—in my handwriting—of an exception to this rule:

One day Livy and Mrs. George Warner were talking earnestly in the library. Susy, who was playing about the floor, interrupted them several times; finally Livy said, rather sharply, "Susy, if you interrupt again, I will send you to the nursery." A little later Livy saw Mrs. W. to the door; on the way back she saw Susy on the stairs, laboring her way up on all fours, a step at a time, and asked—

"Where are you going, Susy?"

"To the nursery, mamma."

"What are you going up there for, dear—don't you want to stay with me in the library?"

Susy was tempted—but only for a moment. Then she said with a gentle dignity which carried its own reproach—

"You didn't speak to me right, mamma."

She had been humiliated in the presence of one not by right entitled to witness it. Livy recognised that the charge was substantially just, and that a consideration of the matter was due—and possibly reparation. She carried Susy to the library and took her on her lap and reasoned the case with her, pointing out that there had been provocation. But Susy's mind was clear, and her position definite: she conceded the provocation, she conceded the justice of the rebuke, she had no fault to find with those details; her whole case rested upon a single point—the *manner* of the reproof—a point from which she was not to be diverted by ingenuities of argument, but stuck patiently to it, listening reverently and regardfully, but returning to it in the pauses and saying gently, once or twice, "But you didn't speak to me *right*, mamma." Her position was not merely well selected and strong—by the laws of conduct governing the house it was impregnable; and she won her case, her mother finally giving the verdict in her favor and confessing that she had *not* "spoken to her right."

Certain qualities of Susy's mind are revealed in this little incident—qualities which were born to it and were permanent. It was not an accident that she perceived the several points involved in the case and was able to separate those which made for her mother from the point which made for herself, it was an exercise of a natural mental endowment which grew with her growth and remained an abiding possession.

Clara Langdon Clemens was born June 8th, 1874, and this circumstance set a new influence at work upon Susy's development. Mother and father are but two—to be accurate, they are but one and a tenth—and they do their share as developers: but along a number of lines certain other developers do more work than they, their number being larger and their opportunities more abundant—i.e. brothers and sisters and servants. Susy was a blonde, Clara a brunette, and they were born with characters to match. As time wore along, the ideals of each modified the ideals and affected the character of the other; not in a large degree of course, but by shades.

Both children had good heads, but not equipped in the same way; Susy, when her spirit was at rest, was reflective, dreamy, spiritual, Clara was at all times alert, enterprising, business-like, earthy, orderly, practical. Some one said Susy was made of mind, Clara of matter—a generalization justified by appearances, at the time, but unjust to Clara, as the years by and by proved. In her early years Clara quite successfully concealed some of the most creditable elements of her make-up. Susy was sensitive, shrinking; and in danger timid; Clara was not shrinking, not timid, and she had a liking for risky ventures. Susy had an abundance of moral courage, and kept it up to standard by exercising it.

In going over the Record which we kept of the children's remarks, it would seem that we set down Susy's because they were wise, Clara's because they were robustly practical, and Jean's because they happened to be quaintly phrased.*

In Susy's and Clara's early days, nine months of the year were spent in the house which we built in Hartford, Connecticut. It was begun the year that Susy was born—1872—and finished and occupied in Clara's birth-year—1874.

In those long-past days we were diligent in the chase, and the library was the hunting-ground—"jungle," by fiction of fancy—and there we hunted the tiger and the lion. I was the elephant, and bore Susy or Clara on my back—and sometimes both—and they carried the guns and shot the game. George, the colored ex-slave, was with us then; first and last he was in our service 18 years, and was as good as he was black—servant,

---

* [*Mark Twain's footnote:*] One evening in the nursery, when Clara was four or five years old and she and Susy were still occupying cribs, Clara was told it was time to say her prayers. She asked if Susy had said hers, and was told she had. Clara said, "Oh, one's enough," and turned over and went to sleep.

By and by, after some months, it was found that Susy had ceased from praying. Upon inquiry it transpired that she had thought the matter out and arrived at the conclusion that it could not be well to trouble God about her small wants, since He knew what they were anyway and could be trusted to reach wise and right decisions concerning them without suggestions from her. She added, tranquilly, "And so I just leave it to Him—He knows."

While Jean was still a little thing, Katy discovered that she was nightly doing some private praying on her own motion after the perfunctory supplications had been disposed of and the nursery vacated by the mamma and other outsiders. These voluntaries were of a practical sort, and covered several important desires: among them a prompt and permanent remedy for stomach-ache. Katy gave us timely notice, and we went up and listened at the door. Jean described the persecutions of her distemper, and added, with strong feeling: "It comes every *day;* and oh, dear Jesus, if you ever had it yourself you would reconnize what it is, and just *stop* it!" "Reconnize" was her largest word, and her favorite. She was the youngest of the children, and came late, comparatively—July 26, 1880.

The Clemenses' Hartford house, 351 Farmington Avenue;
today the Mark Twain House and Museum.

in the matter of work, member of the family in the closer ties and larger enthusiasms of play. He was the lion—also the tiger; but preferably tiger, because as lion his roaring was over-robust, and embarrassed the hunt by scaring Susy. The elephant is left, and one of the hunters; but the other is at rest, and the tiger; and the hunting days are over.

In the early days Patrick McAleer, the coachman, was with us—and had been with us from our wedding day, February 2, 1870. He was with us twenty-two years, marrying soon after he came to us, and rearing eight children while in our service, and educating them well.

Rosa, the German nurse, was a part of the household in the early years, and remained twelve.

Katy was a cotemporary of hers and George's and Patrick's; was with us in Europe twice, and is with us now. To the majority of our old personal friends these names will be familiar; they will remember their possessors, and they will remember, also, that each was an interesting character, and not commonplace.

They would not be able to forget George, the colored man. I can speak of him at some length, without impropriety, he being no longer of this world nor caring for the things which concern it.

George was an accident. He came to wash some windows, and remained half a generation. He was a Maryland slave by birth; the Proclamation set him free, and as a young fellow he saw his fair share of the Civil War as body servant to General Devens. He was handsome, well built, shrewd, wise, polite, always good-natured, cheerful to gaiety, honest, religious, a cautious truth-speaker, devoted friend to the family, champion of its interests, a sort of idol to the children and a trial to Mrs. Clemens—not in all ways but in several. For he was as serenely and dispassionately slow about his work as he was thorough in parts of it; he was phenomenally forgetful; he would postpone work any time to join the children in their play if invited, and he was always being invited, for he was very strong, and always ready for service as horse, camel, elephant or any other kind of transportation required; he was fond of talking, and always willing to do it in the intervals of work—also willing to create the intervals; and finally, if a lie could be useful to Mrs. Clemens he would tell it. That was his worst fault, and of it he could not be cured. He placidly and courteously disposed of objections with the remark—

"Why, Mrs. Clemens, if I was to stop lying you couldn't keep house a week."

He was invaluable; for his large wisdoms and his good nature made up for his defects. He was the peace-maker in the kitchen—in fact the peace-keeper, for by his good sense and right spirit and mollifying tongue he adjusted disputes in that quarter before they reached the quarrel-point. The materials for war were all there. There was a time when we had a colored cook—Presbyterian; George—Methodist; Rosa, German nurse—

Three servants at the Hartford house.
Katy Leary (top left).
Patrick McAleer (top right).
Rosina Hay (left).

Lutheran; Katy, American-Irish—Roman Catholic; Kosloffska, Pole, wet-nurse—Greek Catholic; "English Mary," some kind of a non-conformist; yet under George's benignant influence and capable diplomacy it was a Barnum's Happy Family, and remained so.

There was nothing commonplace about George. He had a remarkably good head; his promise was good, his note was good; he could be trusted to any extent with money or other valuables; his word was worth par, when he was not protecting Mrs. Clemens or the family interests or furnishing information about a horse to a person he was purposing to get a bet out of; he was strenuously religious, he was deacon and autocrat of the African Methodist Church; no dirt, no profanity, ever soiled his speech, and he neither drank nor smoked; he was thrifty, he had an acute financial eye, he acquired a house and a wife not very long after he came with us, and at any time after his first five years' service with us his check was good for $10,000. He ruled his race in the town, he was its trusted political leader, and (barring election-eve accidents) he could tell the Republican Committee how its vote would go, to a man, before the polls opened on election day. His people sought his advice in their troubles, and he kept many a case of theirs out of court by settling it himself. He was well and creditably known to the best whites in the town, and he had the respect and I may say the warm friendly regard of every visiting intimate of our house. Added to all this, he could put a lighted candle in his mouth and close his lips upon it. Consider the influence of a glory like that upon our little kids in the nursery. To them he was something more than mortal; and to their affection for him they added an awed and reverent admiration.

Moreover, he had a mysterious influence over animals—so the children believed. He conferred a human intelligence upon Abner the tomcat—so he made *them* believe. He told them he had instructed Abner that four pressures of the button was his ring, and he said Abner would obey that call. The children marveled, and wanted it tried. George went to the kitchen to set the door open, so that Abner could enter the dining room; then we rang for him, and sure enough he appeared. The children were lost in astonishment at Abner's promptness and willingness, for they had not noticed that there was something about the humping plunge of his entrance that was suggestive of assistance from behind. Then they wondered how he could tell his ring from the other rings—could he count? Probably. We could try experiments and draw conclusions. Abner was removed. Two pressures brought no Abner, it brought Rosa; three brought some one else; five got no response, there being no such ring in the list; then, under great excitement No. 4 was tried once more, and once more Abner plunged in with his suspicious humping impulse. That settled it: Abner could count, and George was the magician that had expanded his intelligence.

"How *did* you do it, George!"

That was the question; but George reserved the secret of his occult powers. His reputation was enlarged; Abner's, too, and Abner's needed it; if any one had gone around, before that, selecting bright cats by evidence of personal aspect, Abner would not have been elected. He was grave, but it was the gravity of dulness, of mental vacancy, his face was quite expressionless, and even had an arid look.

It will not be imagined that George became a moneyed man on his wages of thirty dollars a month. No, his money came from betting. His first speculations in that field were upon horses. It was not chance-work; he did not lay a bet until he knew all that a smart and diligent person could learn about the horses that were to run and the jockeys that were to ride them; then he laid his bets fearlessly. Every day, in the Hartford racing-season, he made large winnings; and while he waited at breakfast next morning he allowed the fact and the amount to escape him casually. Mainly for Susy's benefit, who had been made to believe that betting was immoral, and she was always trying to wean George from it, and was constantly being beguiled, by his arts, into thinking his reform was imminent, and likely to happen at any moment. Then he would fall—and report a "pile" at breakfast; reform again, and fall again before night; and so on, enjoying her irritations and reproaches, and her solemn warnings that disaster would overtake him yet. If he made a particularly rich haul, we knew it by the

ostentatious profundity of his sadnesses and depressions as he served at
breakfast next morning,—a trap set for Susy. She would notice his sadness,
presently, and say, eagerly and hopefully, "It has happened, George, I told
you it would, and you are served just right—how much did you lose?—I hope
ever so much; nothing else can teach you." George's sigh would be ready,
and also his confession, along with a properly repentant look—

"Yes, Miss Susy, I had hard luck—something was wrong, I can't make
out what it was, but I hope and believe it will learn me. I only won eight
hundred dollars."

George reported all his victories to us, but if he ever suffered a loss on
a horse-race we never found it out; if he had a secret of the kind it was not
allowed to escape him, by either his tongue or his countenance.

By and by he added elections to his sources of income. Again he was
methodical, systematic, pains-taking, thorough. Before he risked a dollar
on a candidate or against him, he knew all about the man and his chances.
He searched diligently, he allowed no source of information to escape a
levy. For many years several chief citizens arrived at our house every Friday
evening in the home-season, to play billiards—Governor Robinson, Mr.
Edward M. Bunce, Mr. Charles E. Perkins, Mr. Sam. Dunham, and Mr.
Whitmore. As a rule, one or two of the team brought their wives, who spent
the evening with Mrs. Clemens in the library. These ladies were sure to
arrive in that room without their husbands: because they and the rest of
the gentlemen were in George's clutches in the front hall, getting milked
of political information. Mrs. Clemens was never able to break up this
scandalous business, for the men liked George, they admired him, too, so
they abetted him in his misconduct and were quite willing to help him the
best they could.

He was as successful with his election bets as he was with his turf ventures. In both cases his idea was that a bet was not won until it was won;
therefore it required watching, down to the last moment. This principle
saved him from financial shipwreck, on at least one occasion. He had placed
a deal of money on Mr. Blaine, and considered it perfectly safe, provided

nothing happened. But things could happen, and he kept a watchful eye out, all the time. By and by came that thunderclap out of the blue, "Rum, Romanism, and Rebellion," and Mr. Blaine fell, fatally smitten by the friendly tongue of a clerical idiot. From one of his subsidized information-sources George learned of it three hours before it had gotten currency in Hartford, and he allowed no grass to grow under his feet. Within that time he had covered his Blaine bets out of sight with bets at one to two against him. He came out of that close place a heavy winner.

He was an earnest Republican, but that was a matter to itself; he did not allow politics to intrude itself into his business.

George found that in order to be able to bet intelligently upon State and National elections it was necessary to be exhaustively posted in a wide array of details competent to affect results. Experience presently wrung from him this tardy justice toward me—

"Mrs. Clemens, when I used to see Mr. Clemens setting around with a pen and talking about his 'work,' I never said anything, it warn't my place, but I had my opinions about that kind of language, jist the same. But since I've took up with the election business I reconnize 't I was ignorant and foolish. I've found out, now, that when a man uses these" (holding out his big hands), "it's—well, it's any po' thing you've a mind to call it; but when he uses these" (tapping his forehead), "it's *work*, sho's you bawn, and even *that* ain't hardly any name for it!"

As an instance of what George could do on the turf, I offer this. Once in the summer vacation I arrived without notice in Hartford, entered the house by the front door without help of a latch-key, and found the place silent and the servants absent. Toward sunset George came in the back way, and I was a surprise for him. I reproached him for leaving the house unprotected, and said that at least one sentinel should have been left on duty. He was not troubled, not crushed. He said the burglar alarm would scare any one away who tried to get in. I said—

"It wasn't *on*. Moreover, any one could enter that wanted to, for the front door was not even on the latch. I just turned the knob and came in."

He paled to the tint of new leather, and reeled in his tracks. Then, without a word he flew up the stairs three steps at a jump, and presently came panting down, with a fat bundle in his hand. It was money—greenbacks.

"Goodness, what a start you did give me, Mr. Clemens!" he said. "I had fifteen hundred dollars betwixt my mattresses. But she's all right."

He had been away six days at Rochester, and had won it at the races.

In Hartford he did a thriving banking business in a private way among his people—for a healthy commission. And he lost nothing, for he did not lend on doubtful securities.

I was back, for a moment, in 1893, when we had been away two years in Europe; George called at the hotel, faultlessly dressed, as was his wont, and we walked up town together, talking about "the Madam" and the children, and incidentally about his own affairs. He had been serving as a waiter a couple of years, at the Union League Club, and acting as banker for the other waiters, forty in number, of his own race. He lent money to them by the month, at rather high interest, and as security he took their written orders on the cashier for their maturing wages, the orders including interest and principal.

Also, he was lending to white men outside; and on no kinds of security but two—gold watches and diamonds. He had about a hatful of these trifles in the Club safe. The times were desperate, failure and ruin were everywhere, woe sat upon every countenance, I had seen nothing like it before, I have seen nothing like it since. But George's ark floated serene upon the troubled waters, his white teeth shone through his pleasant smile in the old way, he was a prosperous and happy person, and about the only one thus conditioned I met in New York.

To save ciphering, he was keeping deposits in three banks. He kept his capital in one, his interest-accumulations in another, and in the third he daily placed every copper, every nickel and every piece of silver received by him between getting up and going to bed, from whatever source it might come, whether as tips, or in making change, or even as capital resulting from the paying back of small loans. This third deposit was a sacred thing, the sacredest George had. It was for the education of his sole child, *a little daughter nine months old.*

It had been accumulating since the child's birth. George said—

"It'll be a humping lot by and by, Mr. Clemens, when she begins to need it. I've had to pull along the best I could without any learning but what little I could pick up as I had a chance; but I know the power an education is, and when I used to see little Miss Susy and Miss Clara and Miss Jean pegging away in the schoolroom, and Miss Foote learning them everything in the world, I made up my mind that if ever I had a little daughter I'd educate her up to the eye-lids if I starved for it!"

As I have suggested before, mamma and papa and the governess do their share—such as it is—in moulding a child, and the servants and other unconsidered circumstances do their share; and a potent share it is. George had unwittingly helped to train our little people, and now it appeared that in the meantime they had been as unwittingly helping to train *him.* We—one and all—are merely what our training makes us; and in it all our world takes a hand.

I am reminded that I, also, contributed a trifle once to George's training in the early days there at home in Hartford. One morning he appeared in my study in a high state of excitement, and wanted to borrow my revolver. He had had a rupture with a colored man, and was going to kill him on sight. I was surprised; for George was the best-natured man in the world, and the humanest; and now here was this bad streak in him and I had never suspected it. Presently, as he talked along, I got new light. The bad streak was bogus. I saw that at bottom he didn't want to kill any one—he only wanted some person of known wisdom and high authority to persuade him out of it; it would save his character with his people; they would see that he was properly bloodthirsty, but had been obliged to yield to wise and righteous counsel. So I reserved my counsel; I put new cartridges in the revolver, and handed it to him, saying—

"Keep cool, and don't fire from a distance. Close in on him and make sure work. Hit him in the breast."

He was visibly surprised—and disappointed. He began lamely to hedge, and I to misunderstand. Before long he was hunting for excuses to spare the man, and I was zealously urging him to kill him. In the end he was giving me an earnest sermon upon my depraved morals, and trying to lift me to a higher spiritual level. Finally he said—

"Would *you* kill him, Mr. Clemens? If you was in my place would you, really?"

"Certainly. Nothing is so sweet as revenge. Now here is an insulter who has no wife and no children—"

"Oh, no, Mr. Clemens, he's got a wife and four little children."

I was outraged, then—apparently—and turned upon him and said, indignantly—

"You-u-u—scoundrel! You knew that all the time? Do you mean to tell me that you actually had it in your hard nature to break the hearts and reduce to poverty and misery and despair those innocent creatures for something somebody *else* had done?"

It was George's turn to be staggered, and he was. He said, remorsefully—

"Mr. Clemens, as I'm a standing here I *never* seen it in that light before! I was agoing to take it out of the wrong ones, that hadn't ever done me any harm—I *never* thought of that before! Now, sir, they can jist call me what they want to—I'll stand it."

On our way up town that day in New York I turned in at the *Century* building, and made George go up with me. The array of clerks in the great counting-room glanced up with curiosity—a white man and a negro walking together was a new spectacle to them. The glance embarrassed George, but not me, for the companionship was proper: in some ways he was my equal, in some others my superior; and besides, deep down in my interior I knew that the difference between any two of those poor transient things called human beings that have ever crawled about this world and then hid their little vanities in the compassionate shelter of the grave was but microscopic, trivial, a mere difference between worms. In the first editorial room I introduced "Mr. Griffin" to Mr. Buel and Mr. Johnson, and embarrassed all three. Conversation was difficult. I went into the main editorial room and found Mr. Gilder there. He said—

"You are just the man!" He handed me a type-written manuscript. "Read that first paragraph and tell me what you think of it."

I looked around; George was decamping. I called him back, introduced him to Mr. Gilder, and said—

"Listen to this, George." I read the paragraph and asked him how its literary quality struck him. He very modestly gave his opinion in a couple of sentences, and I returned the manuscript to Gilder with the remark that that was my opinion also. Conversation was difficult again—which was satisfactory to me, for I was there to make an impression. This accomplished, I left, and on my way was gratified to notice that many employes put in a casual appearance here and there and yonder and took a sight of George and me.

Passing the *St. Nicholas* editorial room Mr. Clarke hailed me and said—

"Come in, Mark, I've got something to show you."

I made George come in, too. The thing to be shown was a design for a new cover for *St. Nicholas*. Mr. Clarke said—

"What do you think of it?"

I examined it a while, then handed it without comment to George, introduced him, and asked for his opinion. With diffidence, but honestly, he gave it; I endorsed it, and returned the design to Clarke. Conversation not fluent. Mr. Carey of the general business department appeared, and proposed refreshments. Down in Union Square George dropped behind, but I brought him forward, introduced him to Carey, and placed him between us. There had been a prize fight the night before, between a white man and a negro. Presently I said—

"George, what did you get out of that fight last night?"

"Six hundred dollars, sir."

Carey glanced across me at him with interest, and said—

"Did you bet on the winner?"

"Yes, sir."

"He was the *white* man. Was it quite patriotic to bet against your own color?"

"Betting is business, sir, patriotism is sentiment. They don't belong together. In politics I'm colored; in a bet I put up on *the best man,* I ain't particular about his paint. That white man had a record; so had the coon, but 'twas watered."

Carey was evidently impressed. When we arrived at Carey's refreshment place George politely excused himself and went his way. Presently Carey said—

"What's the game? That's no commonplace coon. Who *is* that?"

I said it was a long story—"wait till we get back to the *Century.*"

There the editorial people listened to the history of George Griffin, and were sorry they hadn't been acquainted with it before he came—they would have "shaken hands, and been glad to; wouldn't I bring him again?"

We sailed for Europe in 1891. Shortly afterward George, concluding that we were not coming back soon—knowing it, in fact—applied for a place at the Union League Club. He was a stranger. He was asked—

"Recommendation?"

He had a gilt-edged one in his pocket from us, but he kept it there, and answered simply—

"Sixteen years in the one family—in Hartford."

"Sixteen years. Then you ought to be able to prove that. By the family, or some known person. Isn't there someone who can speak for you?"

"Yes, sir—anybody in Hartford."

"Meaning everybody?"

"Yes, sir—from Senator Hawley down."

That was George's style. He had a reputation, and he wanted the fact known. There were plenty of Hartford members of the Union League Club, and he knew what they would say. He served there until his death in 1897, faithfully corresponding with the family all the while, and returning with interest the children's affection for him. Susy passed to her rest the year before George died. He was performing his duties in the Club until toward midnight of the 7th May, then complained of a pain at his heart and went to bed. He was found dead in his bed in the morning.

We were living in London at the time. I early learned what had happened, but I kept it from the family as long as I could, the midnight of Susy's loss being still upon them and they being ill fitted to bear an added sorrow; but as the months wore on and no letter came from George in answer to theirs, they became uneasy, and were about to write him and ask what the matter was; then I spoke.

As I have already indicated, Mrs. Clemens and I, and Miss Foote the governess, were in our respective degrees of efficiency and opportunity trainers of the children—*conscious and intentional* ones—and we were reinforced in our work by the usual and formidable multitude of un-conscious and unintentional trainers, such as servants, friends, visitors, books, dogs, cats, horses, cows, accidents, travel, joys, sorrows, lies, slanders, oppositions, persuasions, good and evil beguilements, treach-eries, fidelities, the tireless and everlasting impact of character-forming exterior influences which begin their strenuous assault at the cradle and only end it at the grave. Books, home, the school and the pulpit may and must do the *directing*—it is their limited but lofty and powerful office—but the countless outside unconscious and unintentional trainers do the real work, and over them the responsible superintendents have no considerable supervision or authority.

Conscious teaching is good and necessary, and in a hundred instances it effects its purpose, while in a hundred others it fails and the purpose, if accomplished at all, is accomplished by some other agent or influence. I suppose that in most cases changes take place in us without our being aware of it at the time, and in after life we give the credit of it—if it be of a creditable nature—to mamma, or the school or the pulpit. But I know of one case where a change was wrought in me by an outside influence—where teaching had failed,—and I was profoundly aware of the change when it happened. And so I know that the fact that for more than fifty-five years I have not wantonly injured a dumb creature is not to be credited to home, school or pulpit, but to a momentary outside influence. When I was a boy my mother pleaded for the fishes and the birds and tried to persuade me to spare them, but I went on taking their lives unmoved, until at last I shot a bird that sat in a high tree, with its head tilted back, and pouring out a grateful song from an innocent heart. It toppled from its perch and came floating down limp and forlorn and fell at my feet, its song quenched and its unoffending life extinguished. I had not needed that harmless creature, I had destroyed it wantonly, and I felt all that an assassin feels, of grief and remorse when his deed comes home to him and he wishes he could undo it and have his hands and his soul clean again from accusing blood. One department of my education, theretofore long and diligently and fruitlessly labored upon, was closed by that single application of an outside and unsalaried influence, and could take down its sign and put away its books and its admonitions permanently.

In my turn I admonished the children not to hurt animals; also to protect weak animals from stronger ones. This teaching succeeded—and not only in the spirit but in the letter. When Clara was small—small enough to wear a shoe the size of a cowslip—she suddenly brought this shoe down with determined energy, one day, dragged it rearward with an emphatic rake, then stooped down to examine results. We inquired, and she explained—

"The naughty big ant was trying to kill the little one!"

Neither of them survived the generous interference.

Among the household's board of auxiliary and unconscious trainers, four of the servants were especially influential—Patrick, George, Katy, and Rosa the German nurse; strong and definite characters, all, and all equipped with uncommonly good heads and hearts. Temporarily there was another influence—Clara's wet nurses. No. 1 was a mulatto, No. 2 was half American half Irish, No. 3 was half German half Dutch, No. 4 was Irish, No. 5 was apparently Irish, with a powerful strain of Egyptian in her. This one ended the procession—and in great style, too. For some little time Clara was rich in given-names drawn from the surnames of these nurses, and was taught to string them together as well as her incompetent tongue would let her, as a show-off for the admiration of visitors, when required to "be nice and tell the ladies your name." As she did it with proper gravity and earnestness, not knowing there was any joke in it, it went very well: "Clara Lewis O'Day Botheker McAleer McLaughlin Clemens."

It has always been held that mother's milk imparts to the child certain details of the mother's make-up in permanency—such as character, disposition, tastes, inclinations, traces of nationality and so on. Supposably, then, Clara is a hybrid and a polyglot, a person of no particular country or breed, a General Member of the Human Race, a Cosmopolitan.

She got valuable details of construction out of those other contributors, no doubt; no doubt they laid the foundations of what she is now, but it was the mighty Egyptian that did the final work and reared upon it the imposing superstructure. There was never any wet-nurse like that one—the unique, the sublime, the unapproachable! She stood six feet in her stockings, she was perfect in form and contour, raven-haired, dark as an Indian, stately, carrying her head like an empress, she had the martial port and stride of a grenadier, and the pluck and strength of a battalion of them. In professional capacity the cow was a poor thing compared to her, and not even the pump was qualified to take on airs where she was. She was as independent as the flag, she was indifferent to morals and principles, she disdained company, and marched in a procession by herself. She was as healthy as iron, she had the appetite of a crocodile, the stomach of a cellar, and the digestion of a quartz-mill. Scorning the adamantine law that a wet-nurse must partake of delicate things only, she devoured anything and everything she could get her hands on, shoveling into her person fiendish combinations of fresh pork, lemon pie, boiled cabbage, ice cream, green apples, pickled tripe, raw turnips, and washing the cargo down with freshets of coffee, tea, brandy, whisky, turpentine, kerosene—anything that was liquid; she smoked pipes, cigars, cigarettes, she whooped like a Pawnee and swore like a demon; and then she would go up stairs loaded as described and perfectly delight the baby with a banquet which ought to have killed it at thirty yards, but which only made it happy and fat and contented and boozy. No child but this one ever had such grand and wholesome service. The giantess raided my tobacco and cigar department every day; no drinkable thing was safe from her if you turned your back a moment; and in addition to the great quantities of strong liquors which she bought down town every day and consumed, she drank 256 pint bottles of beer in our house in one month, and that month the shortest one of the year. These things sound impossible, but they are facts. She was a wonder, a portent, that Egyptian.

Patrick the coachman was a part of our wedding outfit, therefore he had been with us two years already when Susy was born. He was Irish; young, slender, bright, quick as a cat, a master of his craft, and one of the only three persons I have had long acquaintance with who could be trusted to do their work well and faithfully without supervision. He was one of the three, I am not the other two—nor either of them. They are John the gardener and his wife—Irish; they were in our service about twenty years.

Patrick, from the earliest days, thirty-six years ago, when he was perhaps twenty-five, carried on his work systematically, competently, and without orders. He kept his horses and carriages and cows in good condition; he kept the bins and the hayloft full; if a horse or a cow was unsatisfactory he made a change; he filled the cellars with coal and wood in the summer while we were away; as soon as a snow-storm was ended he was out with his snow-plow; if a thing needed mending he attended to it at once. He had long foresight, and a memory which was so good that he never seemed to forget anything. In the house, supplies were constantly failing at critical moments, and George's explanation never varied its form, "I declare, I forgotten it"—which was monstrous. This phrase was not in Patrick's book, nor John's.

Patrick rode horseback with the children in the forenoons; in the afternoons he drove them out, with their mother; Susy never on the box, Clara always there, holding the reins in the safe places and prattling a stream; and when she outgrew the situation Jean took it, and continued the din of talk—inquiries, of course; it is what a child deals in. The children had a deep admiration for Patrick, for he was a spanking driver, yet never had an accident; and besides, to them he seemed to know everything and how to do everything. They conferred their society upon him freely in the stable, and he protected them while they took risks in petting the horses in the stalls and in riding the reluctant calves. Also he allowed them, mornings, to help him drive the ducks down to the stream which lazily flowed through the grounds, and back to the stable at sunset. Furthermore, he allowed them to look on and shrink and shiver and compassionately exclaim, when he had a case of surgery on hand—which was rather frequent when the ducks were youthful. They would go to sleep on the water, and the mud-turtles would get them by the feet and chew until Patrick happened along and released them. Then he brought them up the slope and sat in the shade of the long quarter-deck called "the ombra" and bandaged the stumps of the feet with rags while the children helped the ducks do the suffering. He slaughtered a mess of the birds for the table pretty frequently, and this conduct got him protests and rebukes. Once Jean said—

"I wonder God lets us have so much ducks, Patrick kills them so."

A proper attitude for one who was by and by, in her sixteenth year, to be the founder of a branch of the Society for the Prevention of Cruelty to Animals.

Patrick was apt to be around when needed, and this happened once when he was sorely needed indeed. On the second floor of the stable there was a large oat-bin, whose lid shut with a spring. It had a couple of feet of oats in it. Susy, Clara, and Daisy Warner climbed into it, the lid fell and they were prisoners, there in the dark. They were not able to help themselves, their case was serious, they would soon exhaust the air in that box, then they would suffocate. Our house was not close by; Patrick's house was a part of the stable, but between it and the stable were thick walls, muffled screams could not bore through them. We at home in the house were comfortable and serene, not suspecting that an awful tragedy was imminent on the premises. Patrick arrived from down town and happened to step into the carriage house instead of passing along to his own door, as had been his purpose. He noticed dull cries, but could not at once tell whence they proceeded—sounds are difficult things to locate. A stupider man would have gone outside, and lost his head, and hunted frantically everywhere but in the right place; a few minutes of this would have answered all tragic purposes. But Patrick was not stupid; he kept his head and listened, then moved when he had reached a conclusion.

It was not Susy that arranged that scrape, it was Clara; Susy was not an inventor of adventures, she was only an accommodating and persuadable follower of reckless inventors of such things, for in her gentle make-up were no nineteen second-hand nationalities and the evil energies of that Egyptian volcano. Susy took, in its turn, each step of the series that led up to the scrape, but she originated none of them, it was mainly Clara's work, the outcome of her heredities. She was within a day or two of eight years old at the time. Miss Foote required of the children a weekly composition, and Clara utilized the episode in satisfaction of that law. It exhibits Clara's literary gait of that day, and I will copy it here from the original document:

The barn
by
Clara Clemens.

Caught in the Oat Bin, Daisy, Susie and I went up in the barn to play in the hay, there was a great big Oat box up there and I said "Let's get on it" and Daisy said "Yes," so Susie and Daisy pushed me up, Then Susie tried to get up but she could not, I saw a big oil box, and I said "O, Susie take the oil box over there and put it on the steps and you can get on that," and so she did, and they all got up; I began jumping off from it they all were afraid, I was too, at first, And then Daisy said "Let's get in" so I jumped in and then Daisy did; Susie was afraid to get in because she thought there was no bottom to it, but we dug and dug and showed that there was a bottom. So pretty soon she jumped in; then we began to play and pretty soon the cover came down. Then it was roasting hot, in there. Daisy and Susie pushed and I screamed, Patrick thought he heard some one screaming, but he thought we were only playing, still as I kept screaming he thought he would come up and see what was the matter, He found the noise came from the oat box and he opened the lid and let us out, We could not see at all and we felt very hot in there, Patrick said we could have smothered in a little while.

The End.

It is pitiful, those frightened little prisoners struggling, pushing and screaming in the swelter and smother of that pitch-dark hole; I often see that picture and feel the pathos of it. And particularly I feel Susy's fright; that of the others had limits, perhaps, but in such circumstances hers would have none. She was by nature timid; also, she had a forceful imagination. In time of peril this is a powerful combination. The dark closet was never put in Susy's list of punishments; it would have been much too effective. It was tried with Clara, when she was four or five years old, but without adequate results. She was always able to entertain herself, and easily did it in this instance; she did not mind the darkness, and she was the only one that was sorry when the prison-term was up. The Egyptian was probably many times in places similar to that—by request of the State. Susy required much punishing while she was little, but not after she was six or seven years old. By that time she was become a wise and thoughtful small philosopher and able to shut the exits upon her fierce exuberances of temper and keep herself under control. But even Susy's timidity had limits. She was not discomposed by runaways and cab-collisions, and she enjoyed storms and was not afraid of lightning; in a town of the Haute Savoie the night after the assassination of President Carnot, when a mob assailed the hotel with stones and threatened to destroy it unless the Italian servants were delivered into its hands to be lynched, she kept her head. On the other hand sea-voyaging was a torture to her, and a large part of the torture was bred of a constant fear at night that the ship would burn.

Rosa, the German nurse, who was with us ten or twelve years, was a pleasant influence in the nursery and in the house. She had a smart sense of humor, an easy and cordial laugh which was catching, and a cheery spirit which pervaded the premises like an atmosphere. She had good sense, good courage, unusual presence of mind in seasons of danger, and a sound judgment in exercising it. In a hotel in Baden Baden once, when Clara was two years old, and sly and enterprising, and a difficult person to keep track of, an elderly German chambermaid burst into our quarters, pale and frightened, and tried to say something, but couldn't. Rosa did not wait for the woman to find her tongue, but moved promptly out to see for herself what the trouble might be. We were on the third floor. Clara had squeezed her body through the balusters, and was making the trip along them, inch by inch, her body overhanging the vacancy which extended thence to the marble floor three stories below. Rosa did not fly to the child and scare it and bring on a tragedy, but stood at a distance and said in an ordinary voice,

"I have something pretty for thee, Kindchen—wait till I bring it."

Then she walked forward and lifted Clara over the balusters with-out rousing any opposition, and the danger was over for that time. Four years later, at a seaside resort, Clara was drowning, in the midst of a crowd of women and children, who stood paralyzed and helpless and did nothing; Rosa had to run a matter of twenty yards, but she covered the distance in time and saved what was left of the child—a doubtful asset, to all appearances, but, as it turned out, less doubtful than the appearances promised.

Also, Rosa had a two-thirds share in "the Three Days;" the barber had the other third. We were living in the Hartford home at the time, and it was cold weather. Clara had diphtheria, and her crib was in our bedroom, which was on the second floor; over the crib was built a tent of blankets, into which projected the pipe of a steaming apparatus which stood upon the floor. Mrs. Clemens left the room for a little while, and presently Rosa entered on an errand, and found a conflagration; the alcohol lamp had set fire to the tent and the blankets were blazing. Rosa snatched the patient out and put her on the bed, then gathered up the burning mattrass and blankets and threw them out of the window. The crib itself had caught fire; she smothered that detail. Clara's burns were very slight, and Rosa got no burns, except on her hands.

That was the First Day. The next morning Jean, the baby, was asleep in her crib in front of a vigorous wood fire in the nursery on the second floor. The crib had a tall lawn canopy over it. A spark was driven through the close-webbed fire-screen and it lit on the slant of the canopy, and presently the result was a blaze. After a little a Polish servant-woman entered the nursery, caught sight of the tall flame, and rushed out shrieking. That brought Rosa from somewhere, and she rescued the child and threw the burning mattrass and bedding out of the window. The baby was slightly burnt in several spots, and again Rosa's hands suffered, but otherwise no harm was done. Nothing but instant perception of the right thing to do, and lightning promptness in doing it could save the children's lives, a minute's delay in either case would have been fatal; but Rosa had the quick eye, the sane mind and the prompt hand, and these great qualities made her mistress of the emergency.

The next day was the Third Day, and completed the series. The barber came out daily from town to shave me. His function was performed in a room on the first floor—it was the rule; but this time, by luck, he was sent up to the schoolroom, which adjoined the nursery, on the second floor. He knocked; there being no response, he entered. Susy's back was visible at the far end of the room; she was deep in a piano lesson, and unconscious of other matters. A log had burned in two, the ends had fallen against the heavy woodwork which enclosed the fireplace and supported the mantel piece, and the conflagration was just beginning. Five minutes later the house would have been past saving. The barber did the requisite thing, and the danger was over. So ended what in the family history we call "the Three Days," and aggrandize them with capital letters, as is proper.

Rosa was a good disciplinarian, and faithful to her orders. She was not allowed to talk to the children in any tongue but German. Susy was amenable to law and reason, but when Clara was a little chap she several times flew out against this arrangement, and once in Hesse Cassel, with grieved and resentful tears in her eyes, she said to Miss Spaulding,—

"Aunt Clara, I wish God hadn't made Rosa in German."

Rosa was with us until 1883, when she married a young farmer in the State of New York, and went to live with him on his farm. When the young corn began to sprout the crows took to pulling it up, and then an incident followed whose humor Rosa was quite competent to appreciate. She had spread out and stuck up an old umbrella to do service as a scarecrow, and was sitting on the porch waiting to see what the marauders would think of it. She had not long to wait; soon rain began to fall, and the crows pulled up corn and carried it in under the umbrella and ate it—with thanks to the provider of the shelter!

Katy was a potent influence, all over the premises. Fidelity, truthfulness, courage, magnanimity, personal dignity, a pole-star for steadiness—these were her equipment, along with a heart of Irish warmth, quick Irish wit, and a good store of that veiled and shimmering and half-surreptitious humor which is the best feature of the "American" brand—or of any brand, for that matter. The drift of the years has not spirited away any of these qualities; they are her possession still.

Of course there were birds of passage—servants who tarried a while, were dissatisfied with us or we with them, and presently vanished out of our life, making but slight impression upon it for good or bad, perhaps, and leaving it substantially unmodified by their contributions in the way of training. The Egyptian always excepted. And possibly Elise,—a temporary nurse-help for Jean. Elise was a pretty and plump and fresh young maiden of fifteen, right out of a village in the heart of Germany, speaking no language but her own, innocent as a bird, joyous as fifty birds, and as noisy as a million of them. She was sincerely and germanically religious, and it is possible that she did teach us some little something or other—to swear, perhaps. For she had that German gift; and had it in the German way, which does not offend, and is not meant to offend. Her speeches were well larded with harmless handlings of the sacred names. "Allmächtiger Gott!" "Gott im Himmel!" "Heilige Mutter Gottes!" "Nun, schönen Dank, *dass* ist fertig, bei Gott!" "Lieber wäre ich in der Hölle verloren als dass ich dasselbe wieder thun müssen!" "O, Herr Jesus, ja! ich komme gleich!" Apostrophe to the soup, which had burnt her mouth: "Oooh! die gottver-dammte Suppe!"*

Jean, the baby, catching the sound of distant thunder rumbling and crashing down the sky one day, listened a moment to make sure, then nodded her head as one whose doubts are removed, and said musingly—

"That's Elise, again."

One is obliged to like the German profanity, after the ear has grown used to it, because it is so guileless and picturesque and alluring. As winning a swearer as we have known was a Baroness in Munich of blameless life, sweet and lovely in her nature, and deeply religious. During the four months we spent there in the winter of 1878–9, our traveling comrade, Miss Clara Spaulding, spent a good deal of time in her house, and the two became intimate friends. The Baroness was fond of believing that in many pleasant ways the Germans and the Americans were alike, and once she hit upon this happy resemblance:

"Why, if you notice, we even talk alike. We say Ach Gott, and you say goddam!"

The Hartford house stood upon the frontier where town and country met, the one side of the premises being in the town and the other side within the cover of the original forest. The nearest neighbor, in one direction—across the sward with no fence between—was Mrs. Harriet Beecher Stowe; and the nearest neighbors in another direction—through the chestnuts, with no fences—were the Warners (Charles Dudley and

* [*Translations for German profanities:* "Almighty God!" "God in Heaven!" "Holy Mother of God!" "Now, thank goodness *that's* finished, by God!" "I'd rather be damned in Hell than do that over again!" "O, Lord Jesus, yes, I'll be right there!" "Oooh, the goddamned soup!"]

George). Further away were other intimates: John Hooker and Isabella Beecher Hooker, the Norman Smiths, the Perkinses, the Jewells and Whitmores, Rev. Francis Goodwin; Rev. Joseph Twichell (shepherd of our flock and uncle by adoption to the children); Rev. Dr. Burton, Rev. Dr. Parker, Gen. Hawley, Hammond Trumbull, the Robinsons, the Tafts, President Smith of Trinity, the Dunhams, the Hamersleys, the Colts, the Gays, the Cheneys, General Franklin, the Hillyers, the Bunces and so on; and in the very earliest days one had the momentary privilege of a word with the Rev. Horace Bushnell, whose body was failing and his step halting, but his great intellect had suffered no impairment, and in his wonderful eyes the deeps had not shoaled. Now and then the Howellses and the Aldriches and James T. Fields came down from Boston, and Stedman and Bayard Taylor up from New York, and Nasby from Toledo, and Stanley from Africa, and Charles Kingsley and Henry Irving from England, and Stepniak from Russia, and other bright lights from otherwheres. In their several ways, all trainers of the family, and rarely competent! When Susy was twelve years old General Grant described one or two of Sheridan's achievements to her, and gave his reasons for regarding Sheridan as the first general of the age; and later, when she was fifteen or sixteen, Kipling called (at the summer-home near Elmira), and spoke with her and left his card in her hand; and she kept it, and was able to produce it by and by, when Kipling's name shot up out of the unknown and filled the world with its fame.

From all these friends and acquaintances the children unconsciously gathered something, little or much, and it went to the sum of their training, for all impressions leave effects, none go wholly to waste.

"The Farm."

Our summers were spent at "The Farm"—full name, "Quarry Farm"—the home of Theodore and Susan Crane, brother-in-law and sister of Mrs. Clemens. There the children's training was continued by Katy and Rosa, strongly reinforced by John T. Lewis, colored, ex-slave (Mr. Crane's

Mark Twain's study in its original location at Quarry Farm, about 1874. Today the building is on the campus of Elmira College.

farmer), Aunty Cord, colored, ex-slave (cook), David, colored, coachman, and the other Crane servants. Also, there were minor helps: Mr. and Mrs. Crane; Rev. Thomas and Mrs. Beecher, and the Gleasons, half-way down the hill; and the Langdon household at the homestead in Elmira, down in the valley—consisting of one grandmother, and her son Charles and his young family, which young family was of the same vintage as our own.

The house stood seven or eight hundred feet above the valley, and thirteen hundred above sea level, and the view commanded the sweep of the valley, with glimpses and flashes of the river winding through it, the wide-spread town, and the blue folds and billows of the receding Pennsylvanian hills beyond. My study stood (and still stands) on a little summit a hundred yards from the house and at a higher elevation. It was octagonal, glazed all around, like a pilot house, with a sun-protection of Venetian blinds; it had a fireplace, contained a table, a chair and a sofa, and was subject to invasions by the children, but was under quarantine against other wandering people. There was a higher summit, with a furnished tent for these. It was seldom uncomfortably warm at the farm, as it overlooked valleys both in front and behind, and the unobstructed breezes kept the air cool. Every summer we left home for The Farm with great enthusiasm as soon as Clara's birthday solemnities were over. It was always a healthy place. Two of the carriage horses of the early days are hale and serviceable yet, and one of the children's riding-horses, which they rode in almost primeval times is there still, although he was retired on pension years ago and has been a gentleman loafer ever since. This is "Vix," named for Col. Waring's war horse, whose pathetic and beautiful history, as told in the book bearing that title, won the children's worship, and broke their hearts and made them cry; and two of them lived to mourn again when Waring, a finer hero than even his Vix, laid down his life in rescuing Cuba from her age-long scourge of yellow fever—victor and vanquished in one, for he died of the malady himself.

Aunty Cord was six feet high, and nearly twice as black. She was straight and brawny and strong, and had strong notions about things, and a vigorous eloquence in expressing them if the opposing force were "niggers;" for she had no great opinion of "niggers," and was not backward about saying so. She spoke the plantation dialect of Maryland, where she had grown up and produced a little family of slaves before the war. For white folks she had flatteries, the common inheritance of servitude, but none for "niggers." She called Mrs. Clemens "Queen o' de Magazines,"—which was indefinite but sounded fine, and that was enough for Aunty Cord,—and she was even able to invent grand names for me—at half a dollar each. She was expensive, but then she was the only one I could depend upon for such attentions in that over-fastidious household. She petted the children, of course, and also of course she filled their heads with "nigger" superstitions and damaged their sleep, for she had ghosts and witches in stock, and these were a novelty to the children. According to her gospel, a spider in the heart of an apple must be killed, otherwise bad luck will follow; but spiders with cobwebs under the ceiling must be protected from the housemaid's broom, it was bad luck to disturb them. Snakes must be killed on sight, even the harmless ones; and the discoverer of a sloughed snake-skin lying in the road was in for all kinds of calamities. The weather, the phases of the moon, uncanny noises, and certain eccentricities of insects, birds, cattle and other creatures all spoke to her in mystic warnings, and kept her in a fussy state of mind the most of the time. But no matter, she was cheerful, inexhaustibly cheerful, her heart was in her laugh and her laugh could shake the hills. Under emotion she had the best gift of strong and simple speech that I have known in any woman except my mother. She told me a striking tale out of her personal experience, once, and I will copy it here—and not in my words but her own. I wrote them down before they were cold.*

* [Mark Twain's rendering of Mary Ann Cord's story follows, as "A True Story, Repeated Word for Word as I Heard It"—*BG.*]

～～

MARK TWAIN

A True Story, Repeated Word for Word as I Heard It

It was summer time, and twilight. We were sitting on the porch of the farm-house, on the summit of the hill, and "Aunt Rachel" was sitting respectfully below our level, on the steps,—for she was our servant, and colored. She was of mighty frame and stature; she was sixty years old, but her eye was undimmed and her strength unabated. She was a cheerful, hearty soul, and it was no more trouble for her to laugh than it is for a bird to sing. She was under fire, now, as usual when the day was done. That is to say, she was being chaffed without mercy and was enjoying it. She would let off peal after peal of laughter, and then sit with her face in her hands and shake with throes of enjoyment which she could no longer get breath enough to express. At such a moment as this a thought occurred to me, and I said:

"Aunt Rachel, how is it that you've lived sixty years and never had any trouble?"

She stopped quaking. She paused, and there was a moment of silence. She turned her face over her shoulder toward me, and said, without even a smile in her voice:

"Misto C., is you in arnest?"

It surprised me quite a good deal—and it sobered my manner and my speech, too. I said:

"Why, I thought—that is, I meant—why you *can't* have had any trouble. I've never heard you sigh, and never seen your eye when there wasn't a laugh in it."

She faced fairly around, now, and was full of earnestness:

"Has I had any trouble? Misto C., I's gwyne to tell you, den I leave it to you. I was bawn down mongst de slaves—I knows all 'bout slavery, 'case I ben one of 'em my own se'f. Well, sah, my ole man—dat's my husban'—he was lovin' an' kind to me—jist as kind as you is to yo' own wife. An' we had chil'en—seven chil'en—an' we loved dem chil'en jist de same as you loves yo' chil'en. Dey was black, but de Lord can't make no chil'en so black but what dey mother loves 'em an' wouldn't give 'em up, no, not for anything dat's in dis whole world.

"Well, sah, I was raised in ole Fo'ginny, but my mother she was raised in Maryland, an' my *souls!* she was turrible when she'd git started! My *lan'!* but she'd make de fur fly! When she'd git into dem tantrums, she always had one word dat she said. She'd straighten herse'f up an' put her fists in her hips an' say, 'I want you to understan' dat I wa'nt bawn in de mash to be fool' by trash! I's one o' de ole Blue Hen's Chickens, *I* is!'—'case you see dat's what folks dat's bawn in Maryland calls deyselves, an' dey's proud of it. Well dat was her word. I don't ever forgit it, becase she said it so much, an' becase she said it one day when my little Henry tore his wris', awful, an' most busted his head, right up at de top of his forehead, an' de niggers didn't fly aroun' fas' enough to 'tend to him. An' when dey talk' back at her, she up an' she says, 'Look-a-heah!' she says, 'I want you niggers to understan' dat I wa'nt bawn in de mash to be fool' by trash!—I's one o' de ole Blue Hen's Chickens, *I* is!' an' den she clar' dat kitchen an' bandage' up de chile herse'f. So I says dat word, too, when I's riled.

"Well, bymeby my ole mistis say she's broke, an' she got to sell all de niggers on de place. An' when I heah dat dey gwyne to sell us all off at oction in Richmon', O de good gracious I know what dat mean!"

[Aunt Rachel had gradually risen, while she warmed to her subject, and now she towered above us, black against the stars.]

"Dey put chains on us an' put us on a stan' as high as dis poach—twenty foot high—an' all de people stood aroun'—crowds an' crowds. An' dey'd come up dah an' look at us all roun', an' squeeze our arm, an' make us git up an'

walk, an' den say, 'Dis one too ole,' or 'Dis one lame,' or 'Dis one don't 'mount
to much.' An' dey sole my ole man, an' took him away, an' dey begin to sell my
chil'en an' take *dem* away, an' I begin to cry; an' de man say 'Shet up yo' dam
blubberin',' an' hit me on de mouf wid his han'. An' when de las' one was gone
but my little Henry, I grab' *him* clost up to my breas', so, an' I ris up an' says,
'You shan't take him away!' I says; 'I'll kill de man dat tetches him!' I says.
But my little Henry whisper an' say, 'I gwyne to run away, an' den I work an'
buy yo' freedom.' O, bless de chile, he always so good. But dey got him—dey
got him, de men did—but I took an' tear de cloes mos' off of 'em an' beat 'em
over de head wid my chain; an' *dey* give it to *me*, too, but I didn't mine dat.

"Well, dah was my ole man gone, an' all my chil'en—all my seven
chil'en—an' six of 'em I hain't set eyes on agin to dis day—an' dat's twenty-
two year ago las' Easter. De man dat bought me b'long' in Newbern, an' he
took me dah. Well, bymeby de years roll on an' de waw come. My marster
he was a Confedrit Colonel, an' I was his family's cook. So when de Unions
took dat town, dey all run away an' lef' me all by myse'f wid de other niggers
in dat mons'us big house. So de big Union officers move in dah an' dey ask
me would I cook for *dem*. 'Lord bless you,' says I, 'dat's what I's *for*.'

"Dey wa'nt no small-fry officers, mine you, dey was de biggest dey *is*;
an' de way dey made dem sojers mosey roun'! De Gen'l he tole me to boss
dat kitchen; an' he say if anybody come meddlin' wid you, you jist make 'em
walk chalk; don't you be afeard, he say, you's 'mong frens, now.

"Well, I thinks to myse'f, if my little Henry ever got a chance to run
away, he'd make to de Norf, o' course. So one day I comes in dah whah de
big officers was, in de parlor, an' I drops a kurtchy, so, an' I up an' tole 'em
'bout my Henry, dey a listenin' to my troubles jist de same as if I was white
folks; an' I says, 'What I come for is becase if he got away and got up Norf
whah you gemmen comes from, you might a seen him, maybe, an' could
tell me so as I could fine him agin; he was very little, an' he had a sk-yar on
his lef' wris', an' at de top of his forehead.' Den dey look mournful, an' de
Gen'l say, 'How long since you los' him?' an' I say 'Thirteen year.' Den de
Gen'l say, 'He wouldn't be little no mo', now—he's a man!'

"I never thought o' dat befo'! He was only dat little feller to *me*, yit. I never thought 'bout him growin' up an' bein' big. But I see it den. None o' de gemmen had run acrost him, so dey couldn't do nothin' for me. But all dat time, do' *I* didn't know it, my Henry *was* run off to de Norf, years an' years, an' he was a barber, too, an' worked for hisse'f. An' bymeby when de waw come, he ups an' he says, 'I's done barberin',' he says; 'I's gwyne to fine my ole mammy, less'n she's dead.' So he sole out an' went to whah dey was recruitin', an' hired hisse'f out to de Colonel for his servant; an' den he went all froo de battles everywhah, huntin' for his ole mammy; yes indeedy, he'd hire to fust one officer an' den another, tell he'd ransacked de whole Souf—but you see *I* didn't know nuffin' 'bout *dis*. How was *I* gwyne to know it?

"Well, one night, we had a big sojer ball—de sojers dah at Newbern was always havin' balls an' carryin' on. Dey had 'em in my kitchen, heaps o' times, 'case it was so big. Mine you, I was *down* on sich doin's; becase my place was wid de officers, an' it rasp' me to have dem common sojers cavortin' roun' my kitchen like dat. But I always stood aroun' an' kep' things straight, I did; an' sometimes dey'd git my dander up, an' den I'd make 'em clar dat kitchen, mine I *tell* you!

"Well, one night—it was a Friday night—dey comes a whole plattoon f'm a *nigger* ridgment dat was on guard at de house—de house was headquarters, you know—an' den I was jist a *bilin'*! Mad? I was jist a *boomin'*! I swelled aroun', an' swelled aroun',—I jist was a itchin' for 'em to do somefn' for to start me. *An'* dey was a waltzin' an' a dancin'!—*my!* but dey was havin' a time!—an' I jist a swellin' an' a swellin' up! Pooty soon, 'long comes *sich* a spruce young nigger a sailin' down de room wid a yaller wench roun' de wais'; an' roun' an' roun' an' roun' dey went, enough to make a body drunk to look at 'em; an' when dey got abreas' o' me, dey went to kin' o' balancin' aroun', fust on one leg an' den on t'other, an' smilin' at my big red turban, an' makin' fun, an' I ups an' says, '*Git* along wid you!—rubbage!' De young man's face kin' o' changed, all of a sudden, for 'bout a second, but den he went to smilin' agin same as he was befo'. Well, 'bout dis time, in comes

Henry Washington, Mary Ann Cord's son, in later life.

some niggers dat played music an' b'long' to de ban', an' dey *never* could git along widout puttin' on airs. An' de very fust air dey put on dat night, I lit into 'em! Dey laughed, an' dat made me wuss. De res' o' de niggers got to laughin', an' den my soul *alive* but I was hot! My eye was jist a blazin'! I jist straightened myself up, so—jist as I is now—plum to de ceilin', mos'—an' I digs my fists into my hips, an' I says, 'Look-a-heah!' I says, 'I want you niggers to understan' dat I wa'nt bawn in de mash to be fool' by trash!—I's one o' de ole Blue Hen's Chickens, *I* is!'—an' den I see dat young man stan' a starin' an' stiff, lookin' kin' o' up at de ceilin' like he fogot somefn', an' couldn't 'member it no mo'. Well, I jist march' on dem niggers—so—lookin' like a Gen'l—an' dey jist cave' away befo' me an' out at de do'. An' as dis young man was a goin' out, I heah him say to another nigger, 'Jim,' he says, 'you go 'long an' tell de Cap'n I be on han' 'bout eight o'clock in de mawnin'; dey's somefn' on my mine,' he says; 'I don't sleep no mo' dis night. You go 'long,' he says, 'an' leave me by my own se'f.'

"Dis was 'bout one o'clock in de mawnin'. Well, 'bout seven I was up an' on han', gittin' de officers' breakfast. I was a stoopin' down by de stove—jist so—same as if yo' foot was de stove—an' I'd opened de stove do' wid my right han'—so, pushin' it back, jist as I pushes yo' foot—an' I'd jist got de pan o' hot biscuits in my han' an' was 'bout to raise up, when I see a black face come aroun' under mine, an' de eyes a lookin' up into mine, jist as I's a lookin' up clost under yo' face now—an' I jist stopped *right dah,* an' never budged!—jist gazed, an' gazed,—so—an' de pan begin to tremble, an' all of a sudden I *knowed!* De pan drop' on de flo' an' I grab his lef' han' an' shove back his sleeve—jist so, as I's doin' to you—an' den I goes for his forehead an' push de hair back—so—an' 'Boy!' I says, 'if you ain't my Henry, what is you doin' wid dis welt on yo' wris' an' dat sk-yar on yo' forehead!—de Lord God ob Heaven be praise', I got my own agin!'

"O, no, Misto C., *I* ain't had no trouble. An' no *joy!*"

Mark Twain.

～

MARK TWAIN

A Record of the Small Foolishnesses of Susie and "Bay" Clemens (Infants)

"And Mary treasured these sayings in her heart."

[Begun in August at "Quarry Farm" on the Elmira hills—
country residence of Mr. Crane.]
Hartford
1876

Olivia Susan Clemens

was born at the Langdon homestead in Elmira, N.Y., 19th March, 1872 and was named for her grandmother and her aunt Susan Crane.

From early babyhood until she was 3½ years old, she was addicted to sudden and raging tempests of passion. Coaxing was tried; reasoning was tried; diversion was tried; even bribery; also, deprivations of various kinds; also captivity in a corner; in fact, *every*thing was tried that ever had been tried with any child—but all to no purpose. Indeed the storms grew more frequent. At last we dropped every feature of the system utterly and resorted to flogging. Since that day there has never been a better child. We had to whip her once a day, at first; then three times a week; then twice, then once a week; then twice a month. She is nearly 4½ years old, now, and I have only touched her once in the last 3 months. "Spare the rod and spoil the child" was well said—and not by an amateur, I judge.

Susie never had but one nick-name, (a mistake—see below) and only

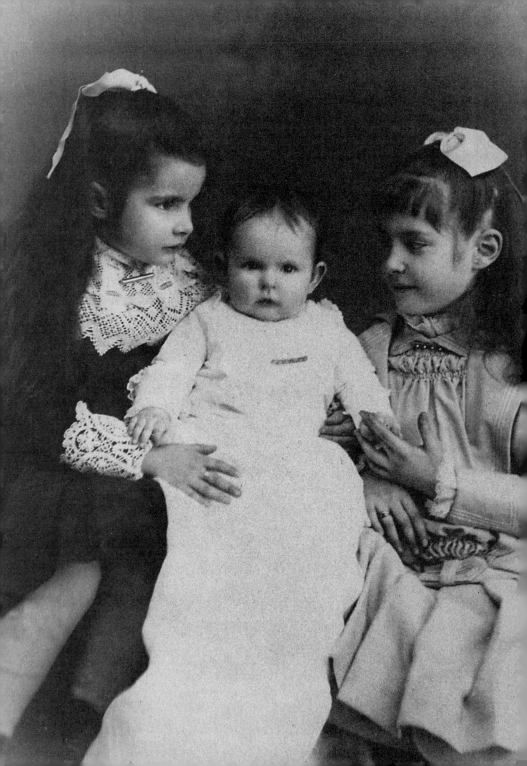

kept that one a year. That was "Modoc," (from the cut of her hair.) This was at the time of the Modoc war in the lava beds of northern California.

Susie began to talk a little when she was a year old. If an article pleased her, she said "*Like* it—awnt (want) it—hab (have) it—*take* it"—and took it, unless somebody got in ahead and prevented.

In the train, on the way from London to Edinburgh (16 months old) she developed a rather lame talent for crowing like a rooster. In Edinburgh her great friend and daily visitor for the 5 weeks we were there was the dearest man in all the land of Scotland—Dr. John Brown, author of "Rab and his Friends." He had two names for her—"Little wifie" and "Megalopis," for her large eyes seemed to him to warrant that sounding Greek epithet. When Susie is an old friendless woman and reads this page, let her remember that she has one thing to be proud of and grateful for—Dr. John Brown loved her and petted her.

Clara Clemens,

(commonly called "the Bay" at this date,) was born at Quarry Farm in the Elmira hills, 8th June 1874, and is 2 years and 2 months old at this writing. She was named for Miss Clara Spaulding, of Elmira, a very especial friend of her parents.

When she was an hour and 4 minutes old, she was shown to Susie. She looked like a velvet-headed grub worm squirming in a blanket—but no matter, Susie admired. She said, in her imperfect way, "Lat bay (baby) got boofu' hair"—so Clara has been commonly called "Bay" to this day, but will take up her right name in time.

When the Bay was a week old, her adventures began. She was asleep on a pillow in a rocking chair in the parlor at Quarry Farm. I had forgotten her presence—if I knew it. I wound up a mechanical toy wagon and set it loose on the floor; I saw it was going to collide with the rocking chair, so I kicked the rocking chair across the house. The Bay lit on the floor with a thump, her head within two inches of the iron fender of the grate, but with the pillow undermost. So she came within 3 inches of an obituary.

From the Bay's first birth-day till some weeks had passed, her chances were uncertain. She could live on nothing but breast milk, and her mother could not furnish it. We got Mary Lewis, the colored wife of the colored lessee of Quarry Farm to supply it a couple of weeks; but the moment we tried to put her on prepared food she turned blue around her mouth and began to gasp. We thought she would not live 15 minutes. Then we got Maggie O'Day from Elmira, who brought her blind child with her and divided up her rations—not enough for the two; so we tried to eke out the Bay's supply with prepared food, and failed. She turned blue again and came near perishing.

We never tried prepared food any more. Next we got Lizzie Botheker, and had to pay her worthless husband $60 to let her come, beside her wages of $5 per week.

Next we got Patrick's wife (our coachman) Mary McAleer to furnish milk for the Bay.

Lastly we got Maria McLaughlin, wife of a worthless Irishman, and she staid a year till the Bay was weaned. Maria chewed, smoked, (swore, used obscene language in the kitchen) stole the beer from the cellar and got drunk every now and then, and was a hard lot in every possible way—but the Bay throve on her vices, right along. So the Bay's name in full is

Clara Langdon Lewis O'Day Botheker McAleer McLaughlin Clemens.

Maria McLaughlin was proprietor of a baby which was boarded at a house on the Gillette place, and by and by it died. Mrs. Clemens gave her $20 out of sympathy and to enable Maria to make a worthy and satisfactory funeral. It had that effect. Maria arrived home about 11 o'clock that night, as full as an egg and as unsteady on end. But the Bay was as empty as *she* was full; so after a steady pull of 20 minutes the Bay's person was level full of milk punch constructed of lager beer, cheap whisky, rum and wretched brandy, flavored with chewing tobacco, cigar smoke and profanity, and the pair were regally "sprung" and serenely happy. The Bay never throve so robustly on any nurse's milk as she did on Maria's, for no other milk had so much substance to it.

We spent the summer of '75 at the seaside at Newport, and the children used to sleep a couple of hours every day under umbrellas on the rocks within six feet of the wash of the waves, and that made them strong and hearty.

Susie began to talk at 1 year, and began to walk in London and perfected herself at 18 months in Edinburgh.

The Bay learned to walk early enough, but now at 2 years and 2 months she cannot say ten words, but understands the entire language.

*

When Susie was nearly 3 years old, I took a spring walk with her. She was drawing a baby carriage with 2 dolls in it, one with a straw hat on. The hat kept falling off and delaying the procession while Susie picked it up. Finally I dropped behind the carriage and said, "Now go on—if it falls off again, I'll pick it up." Nearly 2 days afterward, she said to her English nurse, Lizzy Wills:

"Lizzie, can you talk like papa? When my dolly's hat fell, papa said, 'I-f i-t f-a-l-l-s o-f-f a-g-a-i-n, I---l-l p-i-c-k i-t u-p.'"

Considering that she had probably never heard my drawling manner of speech imitated, this was not bad—nor reverent, either.

*

When Susie Clemens was something over 3 years old, her religious activities began to develop rapidly. Many of her remarks took cast from this interest.

She was found in the act of getting out her water colors one Sunday to make vari-colored splotches and splashes on paper—which she considered "pictures." Her mother said:

"Susie, you forget it is Sunday."

"But mamma, I was only going to paint a few pictures for Jesus, to take up with me when I go."

Susy in 1873, aged seventeen months.

*

Her aunt Sue used to sing a hymn for her which ended—
"I love Jesus because he first loved me."

Susie's mother sang it for her some months afterward, ending it as above, of course. But Susie corrected her and said:

"No, that is not right, mamma—it is because he first loved *Aunt Sue*."
[The word "me" rather confused her.]

*

One day on the ombra Susie burst into song, as follows:

"O Jesus are you dead, so you cannot dance and sing!"

The air was exceedingly gay—rather pretty, too—and was accompanied by a manner and gestures that were equally gay and chipper. Her mother was astonished and distressed. She said:

"Why Susie! Did Maria teach you that dreadful song?"

"No, mamma; I made it myself all out of my own head. *No*-body helped me."

She was plainly proud of it, and went on repeating it with great content.

[Maria McLaughlin was one of Clara Clemens's innumerable wet nurses—a profane devil, and given to whiskey, tobacco, and some of the vices.]

*

1877. Jan. 29

About a fortnight ago Bay got what may be called about her first thrashing. Her mother took both children gravely to the bedchamber to punish them. It was all new to Bay and the novelty of it charmed her. Madam turned Susie across her lap and began to spat her (very lightly.) Bay was delighted with the episode. Then *she* was called for, and came skipping forward with jovial alacrity and threw herself across her mother's lap as who should say, "My, but ain't these good times!" The spat descended sharply, and by the war-whoop that followed, one perceived that the Bay's ideas about these festivities had changed. The madam could not whip for laughing and had to leave the punishment but half performed.

*

1877 January

Mr. Frank D. Millet, the artist, was here to paint my portrait. One day Susie asked her mamma to read to her. Millet said—

"I'll read to you, Susie."

Susie said with a grave sweet grace and great dignity—

"I thank you, Mr. Millet, but I am a little more acquainted with mamma, and so I would rather she would do it."

*

Feb. 15

The other evening, after the children's prayers, Mrs. Clemens told Susie she must often think of Jesus and ask him to help her to overcome bad impulses. She said—

"I do think of him, mamma. Every day I see his cross on my Bible, and I think of him then—the cross they crucified him on—it was too bad—*I was quite sorry.*"

*

Feb. 1877.

The other evening while we were at dinner, the children came down from the nursery as usual to spend the hour between six and seven. They were in the library and the folding doors were open. Presently I heard Susie tell the Bay to lie down on the rug before the fire—which Bay did. Then Susie came into the dining room, turned, ran back, hovered over Bay and said—

"Now, Bay, you are a little dead baby, you know, and I am an angel come down to take you up to heaven. Come, now, get up—give me your hand—now we'll run—that's to pretend to be flying, you know. Ready, now—now we're flying."

When they came flying by the dinner table, something there attracted the Bay's attention and she suddenly stopped, but Susie ran on, full of enthusiasm. She brought up behind a chair by a door and cried out—

"Come on, Bay—here's heaven!"—then put her hand on the door knob and said,—"See! *here's* Jesus!"

*

Mch 15. 1877.

The German letter inserted here* is from Rosa (Rosina Hay,) who has

* [It is missing—BG.]

Library of the Hartford house. Illustration from Harper's New Monthly Magazine, *October 1885.*

been with us since just before Susie's second birth-day—a little over 3 years. Rosa is away on a day or two's visit to New York. She wrote the letter here in Hartford in the nursery and so dated it; but she mailed it today in New York and Susie is very proud of it. Rosa has a very pretty gift at letter-writing.

*

May 4

When Miss Hesse ceased from her office of Private Secretary and took final leave of us today, Susie said gravely, "I am losing all my friends." This is rather precocious flattery.

*

May 4

Yesterday Susie had a present of a new parasol, and hit Bay a whack with it—to see if it was substantial, perhaps. Rosa the nurse took it away from her and put it in the blue room. Susie was vastly frightened and begged Rosa not to tell on her, but her pleadings failed. In the evening Susie said, with earnestness, "Mamma, I begged and begged, and *begged* Rosa not to tell you—*but all in vain.*"

*

May. 77

A month or more ago the Bay was naughty in the nursery and did not finish her dinner. In the evening she was hungry and her mamma gave her a cracker. I quote now from a letter written to me by mamma when I was in Baltimore 2 or 3 days ago:

"Last night, after George had wiped off her sticky fingers in the China Closet, Bay came out with her little sad, downcast look, and said, 'I been litte naughty up 'tairs, can I have a cacker?' [I found that the naughtiness had been invented for the occasion.]"

*

July 4 1877   At the farm.

Susie (being ordered to bed)—said, thoughtfully—"I wish I could sit up all night, as God does."

*

May 1877*

Susie had been a little unreliable in stating facts, I had reproved her quite sharply for it, she went and sat down by herself for sometime and then said "Well mamma I don't know what to do about it,—except that I am sorry and wont do so again"—

*

March 1877—Letter to Mr F. D. Millett from Susie—

Dear Mr Millett

Bay and I has both got valentines, I have a new fan and a German book and bay's got a new carriage—Papa teached me that tick, tick—my Grandfathers clock was too large for the shelf so it stood 90 years on the floor. Mr Millett is that the same clock what is in your picture—Dear Mr Millett I give you my love, I put it on my heart to get the love out. The little Kittye is in Bays carrage my love and Susie Clemens
Write me a little note—

*

Susie trying to work on bristol board failed some what and said "Well Mamma you know the world was not made in a day"—

* [This entry and the two after it were written by Livy—BG.]

*

Susie—4½. Perceiving that her shoes were damaging her feet, from being too small, I got her a very ample pair, of a most villainous shape and style. She made no complaint when they were put on her, but looked injured and degraded. At night when she knelt at her mother's knee to say her prayers, the former gave her the usual admonition:

"Now, Susie—think about God."

"Mamma, I can't, with these shoes."

*

Bay—2 yrs and 2 mos. She can say only a few words; is very fond of rocking and singing—to no tune.

She sings, "*Dee* papa, *dee* mamma, *dee* Do-*ah*, (Theodore Crane), *dee* Tah-*tay* (tante, German for aunt Sue) dee Yo-*wah* (Rosa, German nurse,) dee Shish-*shee* (sister), dee me-e."

It is customary to say "Now, Bay, sing the holy family"—whereupon she performs as above.

Then we say, "Now, Bay, let us have the catechism. Who is a hard lot?"

"Papa."

"Who is a particularly hard lot?"

"Do-ah."

"Who is the hardest lot in Chemung county?"

"Tah-te."

"Who is the hardest lot in the State of New York?"

"Shish-shee."

"Who is the hardest lot in America?"

"Yo-wah."

"Who is the hardest lot in the civilized world?"

"Mamma."

"Who is the confoundedest hardest lot in the entire Universe?"

"Me."

*

Several times Livy said to Susie, "There, there, child, you must not cry for little things." One day (when there was nothing under discussion,) Susie came up out of a brown study with the formidable question, "Mamma, what *is* LITTLE things?" No man can answer that question—nor no woman; for nothing that grieves us can be called little: a child's loss of a doll, and a king's loss of a crown are events of the same size. Livy could not furnish a sufficient answer. But Susie did not give the matter up. She worked at the problem several days. One day, when Livy was about to drive down town— one of her errands being the purchase of a long-promised toy watch for Susie,—the child said, "If you forgot the watch, mamma, would that be a little thing?"

Yet she was not concerned about the watch; for she knew perfectly well it would *not* be forgotten; what the struggling mind was after, was the getting a satisfying grip upon that puzzling question.

*

October 1876 (aged 4 and upwards.)—Susie's mother read to her the story of Joseph. The killing of the kid to stain the garment with blood was arrived at, in due course and made deep impression. Susie's comment, full of sympathy and compassion, was: "*Poor little kid!*" This is probably the only time, in 4000 years, that any human being has pitied that kid—everybody has been too much taken up with pitying Joseph, to remember that that innocent little animal suffered even more violently than he, and is fairly entitled to a word of compassion. I did not suppose that an unhackneyed (let alone an original) thought could be started on an Old Bible subject, but plainly this is one.

*

Aged 4½.—Susie.

Susie repeated a little German stanza about the "Vöglein"; I read it from the book, and with deliberation and emphasis, to correct her pronunciation—whereupon, the Bay, in shattered English, corrected *me*. I said I had read it right, and asked Susie if I hadn't. She said:

"Yes, papa, you did—but you read it so *'stinctly* that it 'fused Bay."

*

Apl. 1877.

Susie said to Miss Alice Spaulding: "I never was at church but once, and that was the day that Bay was crucified." (*Christened.*)

*

Susie has always had a good deal of womanly dignity. One day Livy and Mrs. Lilly Warner were talking earnestly in the library; Susie interrupted them several times; finally Livy said, very sharply,—"Susie, if you interrupt again, I will send you instantly to the nursery!" Five minutes later, Livy saw Mrs. W. to the front door; on her way back she saw Susie on the stairs, and said, "Where are you going, Susie?" "To the nursery, Mamma." "What are you going up there, for, dear?—don't you want to stay with me in the library?" "You didn't speak to me *right*, mamma." Livy was surprised; she had forgotten that rebuke; she pushed her inquiries further; Susie said, with a gentle dignity that carried its own reproach, "You didn't speak to me *right*, mamma." She had been humiliated in the presence of an outsider. Livy felt condemned. She carried Susie to the library, and argued the case with her. Susie hadn't a fault to find with the justice of the rebuke, but she held out steadily against the *manner* of it, saying gently, once or twice, "But you didn't speak to me *right*, mamma." She won her cause; and her mother had to confess that she *hadn't* spoken to her "right."

We require courteous speech from the children at all times and in all circumstances; we owe them the same courtesy in return; and when we fail of it we deserve correction.

*

Munich, (Bavaria,) Nov. 1878.

As we have been traveling for 8 months, this record has been neglected—the book was generally in some trunk that had been sent on ahead. So we will drop *dates* for the present.

*

In Geneva, in September, one morning, I lay abed late, and as Bay was passing through the room I took her on my bed a moment. Then she went to Clara Spaulding and said, "Aunt Clara, papa is a good deal of trouble to me, lately."

"Is he?—Why?"

"Well, he wants me to get in bed with him, and I can't do that with jelmuls (gentlemen)—I don't like jelmuls, anyway."

"What! you don't like gentlemen? Don't you like uncle Theodore?" (Crane)

"O yes—but he ain't a jelmul—he's a *friend.*"

*

To-night she was trying to remind her mother of something, and said—

"It was in Rome—no, Florence,—no, I think it was Venice—or Baden-Baden." Then, after a pause—"*Now* I know!—it was where we saw that kitty."

The moral lies in the fact that she has noticed nothing *but* kitties in all her European travels.

*

Nov. 17 1878.

Susie is sorely badgered with dreams; and her stock dream is that she is being eaten up by bears. Last night she had the usual dream. This morning she stood apart (after telling it) for some time, looking vacantly at the floor and absorbed in meditation. At last she looked up, and with the pathos of one who feels he has not been dealt by with even-handed fairness, said, "But mamma, the trouble is, that I am never the *bear,* but always the

PERSON." (I always give the exact language, in these records.) It would not have occurred to me that there might be an advantage, even in a dream, in occasionally being the eater, instead of always the party eaten, but I easily perceived that her point was well taken.

*

Nov. 30 1878.

This morning, when Bay discovered that this is my birth-day, she was greatly troubled because she had provided no gift for me—repeated her sorrow several times. Finally she went off musing to the nursery and presently returned with her newest and chiefest treasure, a large toy-horse and said, "You shall have this horse for your birth-day, papa." I accepted it with many thanks. After an hour she was racing up and down the room with the horse when Susie said,—

"Why Clara! You gave that horse to papa, and now you've tooken it back again."

Bay.—"I never give it to him for *always;* I give it to him for his *birth-day.*"

*

Munich, Bavaria, Feb. 25, 1879.

Bay finished her little First German Reader, yesterday, and came in with the triumphant announcement: "I'm through, papa! I can read any German book that ever was, now!"

Susie announced, to-day, that she was also through, now, and could read any German book. "And if I can read German books, I can read German papers, too, can't I?" She had the "Allgemeine Zeitung" in her hand, ready to begin. I was obliged to dash her spirits by saying I didn't believe *any*body could read a German newspaper.

However, if the children are a trifle mistaken as to their ability to read German, they certainly speak it as well as they do English, and as glibly and prettily.

We leave for Paris day after tomorrow, to remain several months.

*

May 1879.

Hanover—(stopped there overnight, en route to Heidelberg.) The children had been required, for the past week, to converse with Rosa (the nurse,) in German only. They soon achieved such a hatred for the language that they began to openly rebel and speak to her in English; but she stuck to German in all her replies. This deeply aggravated Bay—and finally she said, "Aunt Clara, I *wish* God had made Rosa in English."

*

March 1879 to Sept 1879

We staid in Paris four months and a half—from the end of February to the middle of July—at the Hotel de Normandie, 7 rue de l'Echelle, corner of the rue St Honoré; then traveled through Holland and Belgium; then spent a few weeks in London and finally reached home the 2d of September, after an absence of nearly a year and a half.

*

Susie made a philosophical remark one day in Paris—in one of her reflective moods—the wording of which I cannot recal; but the exact sense of it was that of the proverb, "It is the unexpected which happens."

*

One day Livy and Clara Spaulding were exclaiming over the odd, queer ways of the French. Susie looked up from her work of doll-dressing and said, "Well, mamma, don't you reckon we seem queer to *them?*"

*

One day in Paris Susie watched her mamma make her toilet for a swell affair at the Embassy, and it was plain that her soul was full of applause, though none of it escaped in words till the last touch was put on and the marvel completed; then she said, with a burst of envying admiration, "I wish *I* could have crooked teeth and spectacles, like mamma!"

*

One day on shipboard a group of ladies and gentlemen began to question Susie as to her relationships; and one lady who felt herself on the track of a kinship with Livy's mother, asked Susie what her grandmamma's name was, before she was married?—which brought out this grave slander, uttered with tranquil simplicity: "My grandmamma has never been married."

*

Remark of Susie's upon having her attention called to some folly or silliness of hers which must have had a bad appearance to the strangers who had been present at the time: "Well, mamma, you know I didn't see myself; so I couldn't know how it looked."—

[The trouble with most of us is that we don't "see ourselves" as others see us, else we would be saved frequent follies.]

*

One evening Susie had prayed; Bay was curled up for sleep; she was reminded that it was her turn to pray, now; she said, "O, one's enough!" and dropped off to slumber.

*

Once in Paris we found that Susie had about ceased from praying. The matter was inquired into. She answered, with simplicity: "I hardly ever pray now; when I want anything, I just leave it to Him—He understands."

[The words, without her voice and manner, do not convey her meaning. What she meant, was, that she had thought the thing all out, and arrived at the conclusion that there was no obstructing vagueness or confusion between herself and God requiring her to explain herself in set words;—when she felt a want, He knew it without its being formulated, and could be trusted to grant or wisely withhold as should be best for both parties; and she was conscious of the impropriety and the needlessness of bothering Him with every little craving that came into her head.]

*

One day, at home, Livy borrowed a little Japanese fan, of Susie, on the ombra—(a trifle that cost 5 cents;) but kept returning it after every two-minutes use of it, saying "That will do for the present, thank you, Susie." But Susie is deep. She knew mamma would use the fan all the time except that she would not allow herself to deprive *her* of her plaything; so she went for her money-box and persuaded Patrick, (the coachman,) to leave his work and go down town—a mile and a half—and buy a similar fan for mamma to have all to herself. It was a thoughtful attention, and delicately done. She kept her secret till the thing was accomplished; for she knew that otherwise mamma would insist upon paying for the fan herself. [And it was characteristic of Patrick, too, to tramp three miles to humor the child's kindly whim.]

*

Susie *is* singularly thoughtful. She often makes me blush for my distinguished lack of that quality. Many a time I have proposed to her some dazzling enterprise which I expected her to jump at with delight, and have been shot down with the remark: "But papa, you know mamma does not allow us to do that." Perfectly true, but I had forgotten it—for the moment. She and Bay will have every right to remember their mother with pride, and speak of her with affection and reverence, as long as they live; for their rearing, under her hands, has been a master-work of good sense, sound judgment, loving consideration, and steady, even-handed justice. They never have known what it was to owe allegiance to, and be the shuttle-cock of, a capricious fool in petticoats, who is all sugar one moment and all aqua-fortis the next; who thrashes for a misdemeanor to-day which she will allow to pass tomorrow; who requires obedience by fits and starts, and puts up with the opposite between-times. No—this description, which fits more or less closely the vast majority of mothers, does not fit theirs in any part. Their mother has always kept faith with them; they could always depend upon her; they never could doubt her. When she promised them a punishment or a present, they knew it was just as sure to come as if the Angel of Fate had spoken it; they knew that all her promises were as good as gold, for she never told them a lie, nor ever beguiled them with a subterfuge. They also knew that she never punished in revenge, but in love; and that the infliction wrung her mother-heart, and was a sore task to her. Let them bless her more for those punishments, whilst they live, than for her gifts; for she was born to give, and it cost her no pang; but to deal out penalties was against her nature; but she *did* deal them out, firmly and unflinchingly, for the great love she bore her children. Mothers have all sorts of formulas: "Do that, or I will punish you;" "If you do that again, I will punish you;" "If you will do so-and-so, I will give you something nice, by and by"—and so on; and still the child disobeys, persistently, and nothing comes of it; for the child has learned that the promise of punishment will not be kept, and that the promised "nice thing" will be given *anyhow*, for the sake of peace. Livy's formula was simply "Do this"—and it had to be done. It was kindly and gently spoken, but it admitted of no deflection from the exact performance. She is a perfect mother, if ever there was one.

One day a neighbor of ours whose children never obey her except when it suits them, begged Susie and Bay to come in and see her (they were in her grounds.) They declined, and said mamma had told them (at some time or other) not to go into a house without her permission—thus intimating their knowledge that although the command had not lately been repeated, it was still in force and must be respected until it was distinctly abrogated. This ought to have compelled this lady's admiration; on the contrary she heedlessly set herself to work to *persuade* the children to come in, against their consciences—saying *she* would take all the responsibility,

etc., and at last won their reluctant acquiescence; she took all this trouble
to undermine a foundation of obedience which had been laid at such
protracted and pains-taking cost. I never can think of this outrage and
keep my temper. However, at the end of two minutes she found that the
children were so full of doubts and misgivings, and so ill at ease that they
were far from enjoying themselves—so she let them go. This lady is one
of the noblest and loveliest spirits in the land, but she is no more fitted to
govern children than she is to govern the Indians.

*

Quarry Farm, July 1880.

The children have been taught to conceal nothing from their mother.
They have been taught to come to her and confess their misdeeds, explain
how the whole thing was, and trust the matter of the punishment to her,
knowing that her perfect fairness can always be relied on. Well, hay-cutting
time was approaching, and for days the children were in a state of vast
excitement; because, for the first time in their lives they were going to be
allowed to embark in the prodigious adventure of a ride to the barn on the
summit of a load of hay. It was all the talk. The hay was cut at last—next day
it would be hauled! And now came Susie with a confession; she had been
doing something of superlative naughtiness—she had struck Bay, I think.
But no matter what it was. Her mother followed her invariable custom—
took the child to a private room to talk the matter over—for she never
inflicts punishment until she has made the culprit understand its fault and
why it is punished. At the end of the talk, this time, Susie comprehended
her crime, and acknowledged that it was of very serious magnitude. A
punishment of corresponding size had to be devised; so upon this work
mamma began, and took Susie into the matter, also, as a kind of consulting
counsel. Various penalties were canvassed and discussed—among them,
deprivation of the hay-wagon ride—and this one manifestly hit Susie the
hardest of all. By and by there was a summing up, and mamma said, "Well,
Susie, which one do you think it ought to be?" Susie studied a while, and

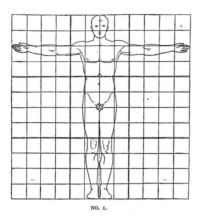
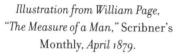

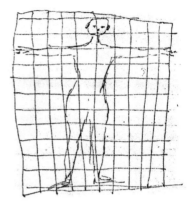

Illustration from William Page,
"The Measure of a Man," Scribner's
Monthly, *April 1879.*

Mark Twain's rendering of same,
from the "Small Foolishnesses"
manuscript.

said, "Which do *you* think, mamma?" "Well, Susie, I would rather leave it to you—you make the choice yourself." After a deal of deep thought, Susie got the thing all weighed out satisfactorily in her mind, and said, "Well, mamma, I will make it the hay-wagon; because you know, mamma, the other things might not make me remember not to do it again; but if I don't get to ride on the hay wagon, I can remember *easily.*" [They perfectly understand that the main purpose of punishment is to make them remember to not commit the fault again.] Poor child! anybody's natural impulse would be to jump up in a gushy way and say "Go free! your Spartan fidelity to the bitter task laid upon you has won your pardon." I do not know what Livy did, but I judge she did not do that. Firstly, she would not be likely to establish the precedent of allowing a just and honorable compact to be departed from; and secondly, since she was distinctly trying to contrive a punishment which would make Susie *remember,* she would not be likely to throw it aside from a mistaken generous impulse and leave her in a position to go and commit the fault again.

*

In Paris, when my day's writing, on the 6th floor, was done, I used to slip quietly into our parlor on the 2d floor, hoping to have a rest and a smoke on the sofa before dinner was brought up; but I seldom succeeded, because the nursery opened into the parlor, and the children were pretty sure to come in for something and discover me—then I would have to take a big chair, place a child on each arm of it, and spin them a story. Whenever Bay discovered me she always called out (without any preliminary by-your-leave) "Susie, *come!*—going to have a story!" Without any remark to me she would go and get a magazine, perch herself on the chair-arm, seek out a suggestive picture, (Susie taking perch on the other arm, meantime), then say, "We're ready, papa."

The tough part of it was, that every detail of the story had to be brand-new—invented on the spot—and it must *fit the picture*. They wouldn't have the story that already belonged to the picture, nor any part of it, nor even any idea that was in it; they were quick to discover when I was borrowing a suggestion from the book, and then they would immediately shut down on that irregularity. Sometimes they would take such a strong fancy to one particular picture that I would have to build an entirely new story upon that picture several evenings in succession. Their selections were pretty odd, too, sometimes. For instance, in the back part of a "Scribner's Monthly" they once found an outline figure which Page the artist had drawn to show the just proportions of the human frame. (See preceding page.) The chances of getting anything romantic, adventurous and heroic out of so sterile a text as that, seemed so remote, that I tried to divert them to a more promising picture; but no, none but this one would answer. So I bent myself to my task; and made such a thrilling and rattling success of it that I was rewarded with the privilege of digging a brand-new story out of that barren text during the *five ensuing evenings*. I wore that poor outline devil's romantic-possibilities entirely out before I got done with him. I drowned him, I hanged him, I pitted him against giants and genii, I adventured him all through fairy-land, I made him the sport of fiery dragons of the air and the pitiless monsters of field and flood, I fed him to the cannibals. The cross-bars which intersected him were the iron gratings of a dungeon in one story, the web of a gigantic spider in another, the parallels of latitude and meridians of longitude webbing a vast and helpless denizen of the wandering comets—and so on; for it was rigidly required of me that those cross-bars be made to play a big and essential role in every yarn.

In all my inventions for the children, from that day to this, I have always had one formidable difficulty to contend with—my villains *must not lie.* This hampered me a good deal. The blacker and bloodier and viler I painted the villain of my tale, the more the children delighted in him, until he made the mistake of telling a lie—then down he went, in their estimation. Nothing could resurrect him again; he simply had to pack up and go; his character was damaged beyond help, the children wouldn't have him around, any longer.

Sometimes I tried to cover up, or slide over, or explain away, one of these lies which I had blundered into, but this was lost time, for Susie is an alert critic. I was calmly proceeding, one evening: "But the moment the giant invited him, the grasshopper whispered in Johnny's ear that the food was poisoned; so Johnny said, very politely, 'I am very much obliged to you indeed, sir, but I am not hungry,—'" "Why *papa!* he told a *lie!*" [Consound that blunder! I said to myself—I must try to get Johnny out of this scrape.] "Well, you see, Susie, I reckon he didn't think what he was saying, and—" "But papa, it couldn't *be*—because he had just said, that very minute, that he was *so* hungry!" "Yes, that is true—yes, that is so—well, I think perhaps he was heedless, and just came out with the first thing that happened in his mind, and—" "O, no, papa, he wasn't ever a heedless boy; it wasn't like him to be heedless; you know how wise he always was—why night before last, you remember"—(this was a *continued* story, which lasted over a week)—"when all those fairies and enchanted creatures tried their very best, a whole day, to catch him in some little carelessness so they could get power over him, they never *could*—no, as long as this story has gone on, papa, there never was such a wise boy before—he *couldn't* be heedless, papa." "Well, Susie, I reckon he was so weary, so kind of tired out—" "Why papa, he *rode* all the way, on the eagle, and he had been sound asleep all the whole day in the gold and ivory bed, with his two lions watching him and taking care of him—why how *could* he be tired, papa, and he so strong?— you know the other night when his whale took him to Africa he went ashore and walked all day and all night, and wasn't a bit tired—and you know that other time when—" "Yes, yes, you are right, Susie, and I was wrong; he couldn't have been tired—but he never intended any wrong; I'm sure he didn't mean what he said; for—" "Then it *was* a lie, papa! if he didn't mean what he said."

Johnny's days of usefulness were over; he was up a stump, and I had to leave him there. The children are good listeners, generally; they do not interrupt—to criticise—until somebody lies. Then the interruptions come thick and fast. They will put up with all inconsistencies in my people cheerfully but that solitary *one;*—that even the blackest scoundrel should lie, is out of character, inconsistent, inexcusable; and the children are bound to call him to the strictest account every time.

They did not get this prejudice from me.

Bay is a sturdy little character; very practical, precious little sentiment, no nonsense. She is sensitive, and can be deeply hurt; I think she must have been 5 years old (she is 6, now), before we discovered this fact—at least before we realized it. This, I think, was because she has the power of concealing all but the big hurts: a power born of her high pluck and fortitude. Pluck and fortitude have been marked features of her character from the beginning; they were born in her—they had to be educated into Susie, who has them, now, (8⅓ years old) in a pretty considerable degree but was born destitute of them. When Bay used to toddle out to feed the fowls, they would swarm around her, and all over her, a greedy, struggling horde, and trip her up or buffet her down, occasionally—all of which she enjoyed—but Susie used to fly. Bay did not mind the electric shocks from the bell-buttons, on cold mornings, but they frightened Susie. Bay (at 3) would hold Japanese fireworks in her fingers till they flashed and spit and sputtered all away—but when the angry volume of sparks began to storm around Susie's hand, she would presently back down and let go. The children's hands were always full of slivers—it was distressing and exasperating to observe Susie's poltroonery under the operation of removing them; it was mere entertainment to Bay to have *her* slivers dug out. When Bay was 3, she had the end of her forefinger crushed nearly off— she was full of interest and comment while the doctor took his stitches, and hardly winced. In Europe, Susie was shy of crowds of strangers, and hung back in the shelter of the party whenever we arrived at a new town and its big inn; but Bay always marched far in the lead and alone, and tramped up the steps and invaded those hotels with the air of a proprietor taking possession. Bay is not without a certain degree of pride in her fortitude. Last spring she had an angry and painful boil on her hand, and mamma made preparation to cut into it. Bay was serene, Susie was full of tremors and anxieties. As the cruel work progressed, Bay was good grit, and only winced, from time to time. Susie kept saying, "*Isn't* she brave!"—and at last a compliment was even wrung from mamma, who said, "Well you *are* a brave little thing!" Bay placidly responded, "*There ain't anybody braver but* God!"

Under mamma's teachings and Bay's example, Susie is making most gratifying progress. Last week she allowed a tooth to be pulled, and was as steady and tranquil about it as any grown person could have been; yet the forceps slipped off it three or four times before the doctor achieved success.

Both of the children are sweet, gentle, humane, tractable, and lovable creatures, with sharply marked and differing characters, with thunder and lightning between—in the spaces. Susie is intellectual, a deep thinker, is analytical, and a reasoner—is a philosopher, too. We had always looked upon Bay as a mere and dear little animal; but lately we are beginning to suspect that she has a mind, and that she is deep, and thinks out problems in privacy and keeps the results to herself. We shall see, by and by. These children are selfish and high-tempered, naturally—but they have been so long and so diligently taught to keep these two gifts under the governance of a taut rein, that they do not show out very frequently.

Susie is an admirable character. There is not a coarse fibre in her; she is as fine as gossamer. She was born free of selfishness—a thing I was not glad of, for a little of it is not only valuable, but a *necessary* quality in every rightly-constructed human creature—but Bay had a noble share, and has divided up with her in the most generous way—so both are just about rightly equipped, now. Susie has an unusually penetrating mind, a charitable spirit, and a great heart. It is curious (and there's a pang in it, too,) to see so little a creature struggling to sound the great deeps of thought with her brief plummet, and groping among the mighty mysteries of life with her poor little farthing candle. Some sayings of hers, jotted down here and there in this book are the outcome of what were reveries and thinkings at times when long stillnesses on her part led us to suppose she was absorbed with her dolls:

"Mamma, what *is* LITTLE things?"

"Papa, how will brother Langdon know us, in heaven?—it is so long that he has been there; and he was such a little fellow."

"Mamma, what is it all for?" (life, labor, misery, death, etc.)

"Mamma, do we walk ourselves, or is it our bodies that are alive?" (Meaning, do our muscles act of their own volition, or is the impulse communicated to them by some higher authority in us?)

(After struggling with the fact that rain and sea are water, and yet not the same—a deep mystery)—"I find there are a great many things that I don't understand, mamma."

These remarks belong to the age of 2½ up to 5; there were plenty more, but they were not recorded, and have passed from memory.

A few days ago she asked a few questions which showed that she had discovered that life and death and suffering and toil and worry simply go on and on and on; forever repeating themselves; striking out nothing new or fresh; ending always in futile ashes and mystery—no perceptible result; at least no result worth all this trouble. Then she had a long reverie over the matter, and finally said—

"Mamma, what does the world go on, for?"

I wish I could recal some of Susie's speeches which illustrate her discriminating *exactness* in the matter of expressing herself upon difficult and elusive points, for they have often been remarkable—some of them were as good, in the matter of discriminating between fine shades of meaning, as any grown person could turn out.

Even Bay is beginning to avoid looseness of statement, now, and to lean toward an almost hypercritical exactness. The other day she was about to start on an excursion among the calves and chickens in the back enclosure, when her Aunt Sue, feeling compassion for her loneliness, proposed to go with her. Bay showed a gratification of so composed a nature that it was hard to tell it from indifference, with the naked eye. So aunt Sue added— "That is, if you would be happier to have me go——would you be happier?" Bay turned the thing over in her mind a couple of times, to make sure, then said, "Well—I should be *happy,* but not HAPPIER."

One couldn't ask to have a thing trimmed any finer than that, I think.

*

Aug 1. 1880.

Susie was sick all day, up stairs, but was brought down to her mother's bedside this evening for a few minutes. Mamma said, "I have missed you so—have you missed me, Susie?" Susie remained silent, and weighed the matter, with the conscientious desire to frame a reply which should convey the exact truth, no more, no less. When she had got it thought out and *knew* she knew how the matter stood in her mind and feelings, then this modern young George Washington who cannot lie, said: "Well—no—I had Aunt Sue and Rosa with me all the time; and they talked, and papa read to me a good deal—no, I did not miss you, mamma." It was very sweetly and simply said: the *manner* of it could wound no one. Mamma said afterward that the *fact* broke her heart a little, at the moment, but that at the same time she respected and honored the child for her dauntless truthfulness. [Now mamma shouldn't have had any pang at all; for she knew Susie loved her to desperation, and did not miss her for the mere reason that her mind had been kept occupied with other things all the time. She has taught Susie to speak the absolute truth, unembroidered and ungilded; and Susie doesn't know how to tell any other kind of a truth.]

We often *commend* the children, of course, when they have been good, but never in such a way as to make them vain and boastful. We *never* tell to other people the fine things they have said or done when they are within hearing—as less wise and extraordinary parents are so given to doing; and although they *are* beautiful, we are particular not to mention that fact in their presence. But the other day, when Susie's tooth was pulled, Bay overheard some of the praises of her fortitude; and consequently has been aching to have a tooth pulled herself, ever since. She has been trying daily (but without success) to convince us all that one of her teeth is loose. But yesterday when Susie developed *two* decidedly loose teeth, poor Bay gave it up in despondency and despair: it was no use to try to buck against such odds as that. Aug 2. 1880

Which reminds me that when Bay was 3 years old, Susie was taken down to the town, one day, and was taken with a vomiting when she got back in the evening. Bay, off in the corner in her crib—totally neglected— observed the coddling and attention which Susie was receiving, as long as she could reasonably stand it; then sat up and said grandly and simply: "Well, some time *I* be dressed up and go down town and come back and throw up, too."

*

Aug. 28, 1880—Poor little Jean frightens herself nearly out of her skin in most odd and rather unmentionable way (she 5 weeks old.)

*

About the 18th or 20th of Oct./80, Bay (who has never been allowed to meddle with English alphabets or books lest she would neglect her German), collared an English juvenile-poem book sent her from London by Joseph the courier—and *now,* 10 or 12 days later (Oct. 30) she reads abstruse English works with an astounding facility! Nobody has given her an instant's assistance. Susie has learned to read English during these same 10 or 12 days, but she is 8 yrs old, and besides she can't read it as glibly as Bay.

*

Random Notes.
Oct. 1880.

During *ten days* of this month, Bay and Susie *taught themselves to read English, without help or instruction from anybody, and without knowing the alphabet,* or making any attempt to *spell* the words or divide them into syllables.

*

Dec. 1880.

They both read fluently, now, but they make no attempts at spelling; neither of them knows more than half the letters of the alphabet. They read wholly by the *look* of the word. Bay picks up any book that comes handy—seems to have no preferences.—The reason they have learned to read English and are so fond of it, is, I think, because they were long ago forbidden to meddle with English books till they should be far advanced in German. Forbidden fruits are most coveted, since Eve's time.

*

7th Dec. 1880.

Bay and Susie were given candy this morning for not having quarreled yesterday—a contract of long standing. Bay began to devour hers, but Susie hesitated a moment, then handed hers back, with a suggestion that she was not fairly entitled to it. Mamma said, "Then what about Bay?—she must have quarreled too, of course." Susie said, "I don't know whether Bay felt wrong in her heart, but I didn't feel right in my heart."

Susie made a pretty nice distinction here—she had kept the *letter* of the contract to not quarrel, but had violated the spirit of it; she had felt the angry words she had not spoken.

No, I got it wrong. Susie meant that Bay's talk might have been only chaff and not ill-natured; she could not tell, as to that; but she knew her own talk came from an angry heart.

*

The last day of the year 1880.

For some months Bay has been bribed to not quarrel with Susie—at 3 cents a day. Conversation to-day:

Bay. "Mamma, you owe me for two days."

Mamma. "Bay, you have not seen Susie for 2 days—she has been sick in bed."

Bay. "Why Mamma, don't you count that?"

*

1881

Susie (9 yrs old,) had been sounding the deeps of life, and pondering the result. Meantime the governess had been instructing her about the American Indians. One day Mamma, with a smitten conscience, said—

"Susie, I have been so busy that I haven't been in at night lately to hear you say your prayers. Maybe I can come in tonight. Shall I?"

Susie hesitated, waited for her thought to formulate itself, then brought it out:

"Mamma, I don't pray as much as I used to—and I don't pray in the same way. Maybe you would not approve of the way I pray now."

"Tell me about it, Susie."

"Well, mamma, I don't know that I can make you understand; but you know, the Indians thought they knew: and they had a great many gods. We know, now, that they were wrong. By and by, maybe it will be found out that *we* are wrong, too. So, now, I only pray *that there may be a God—and a heaven*—OR SOMETHING BETTER."

It was a philosophy that a sexagenarian need not have been ashamed of having evolved.

*

April 1882

The children have been devoting themselves to charades, lately, with prodigious enthusiasm. The other day, Bay came to Miss Spaulding, in a state of excitement, and said she had thought out a good word for a charade—said the word was "register."

"How are you going to act it, Bay?"

"Well, Susie and I will come into the library, from the hall, and talk a good deal of talk about *colors*—but we won't say anything about *red*—only *colors,* that's all. Then we will go out and come in again, and be all the time talking about something that's *just,* or *ain't* just. Next we'll come in talking about a girl, but we won't ever say *her,* but always say *she.*" [Red—just—her—*register!*]

And they gravely played it that way, that night, and were vastly gratified to see how promptly we guessed it.

*

Mem.

July 1882. Susie 10 years old. Came to mamma's room and asked if she should ring for the nurse: Jean, in the nursery, was crying. Mamma asked, "Is she crying *hard?*" (meaning, cross or ugly.) "Well, no—it's a weary, lonesome cry."

She is growing steadily into an admirably discriminating habit of language. Yes, and into the use of pretty large words, too, sometimes—as witness: The night before, I referred to some preference expressed by Jean. Susie wanted at once to know *how* she expressed it—inasmuch as Jean knows only about a dozen words. I said, "Why she spoke up, with marked asperity, and exclaimed, 'Well, Mr. Clemens, you may support that fallacy, if native perversity and a fatuous imagination so move you; but the exact opposite is my distinct and decided preference.'"

Susie's grave eyes stood wide open during this speech; she was silent a moment to let it soak home, then said in a tone of absolute conviction, "Well, papa, that *is* an exaggeration!"

*

Mem.

Once when Bay was 3 or 4 years old, she said, "Mamma, I brang you these flowers"—paused, then corrected herself—"No, I *brung* them."

*

July 1882. Elsewhere I have spoken of Susie's proclivity for large words. The other day Bay crept behind Clara Spaulding's chair, and nearly succeeded in touching her cheek with a wet little wee turtle. Clara S. gave a slight scream, and Susie (who was watching,) was racked and torn with laughter—and said: "Aunt Clara, if it had actually touched your cheek, I should have been *transformed!*" [Meant transported—with glee.]

*

July, 1882. Jean is two years old, now, and brokenly says a few dozen disconnected words, half of them German and the other half English.

*

Dec. 1. '82. Clara 8 years old last June.

AN ACTOR'S FATAL SHOT.

CINCINNATI, Nov. 30. 1882—This afternoon at the Coliseum theater, in the fourth act of the play "Si Slocum," Frank Frayne, in shooting the apple off the head of *Lucy Slocum*, personated by Miss Annie Van Behren, missed the apple and shot Miss Van Behren in the head. She died in fifteen minutes. Frayne was immediately arrested. The curtain fell and the play was stopped. The audience supposed the victim was only slightly hurt. Frayne used a Stevens' rifle, No. 22 calibre, and was executing his backward shot. The catch snap of the rifle was imperfect and slipped just as the hammer fell, blowing the cartridge shell out backwards.

When the curtain went down after the fatal shot, the excitement behind the scenes was so great as to create alarm lest a panic might ensue among the audience of 2,300. Frayne's cries and lamentations were so violent that he was heard before the curtain. Manager Fennessey was too much excited to say anything, but he sent a friend to the front to say that the accident was slight and that the play would not proceed further. The audience then retired in order, although one lady fainted. Manager Fennessey took charge of Frayne, and though the latter demanded to be locked up, he got Mr. H. H. Erick to go before Judge Higley, of the police court, and give a bond for his release from arrest. The bond was fixed at $3,000. Frayne's mental condition was such that one or two of his friends kept close watch over him at his hotel. The theater is closed for to-night and probably will not be opened this week. The coroner viewed the body of Miss Van Behren and it was then removed to Undertaker Habig's where it will lie until word is received from her friends in Brooklyn. It is said that she was engaged to be married shortly to Frayne.

The above telegram was read at breakfast this morning and the fearful scene in the theatre discussed. Then there was a pause of horror. Clara, whose thoughts were with the poor actor, broke it with this remark, uttered with cast-iron gravity:

"I should think he would have been embarrassed."

She was immortally embarrassed, herself, when she perceived by the resulting burst of laughter, that she had got the wrong word by the tail.

*

Dec. 1882.

Jean, 2½ years old, now, talks a lot of rot, in German and English, badly mixed. She says nothing original or reportable, however. Calls herself "Besshy Mish Chain" (Blessed Miss Jane), and "Deedo fen" (Theodore's friend.) She also calls herself "*Asshu* cumbit" (Aunt Sue's comfort.) There's considerable music in it (to us,) when, as she starts down at 6 p.m., we call out to know who's coming, she answers from the unseen remotenesses of the head of the stairs, "Besshy Mish Chain coming, Mamma."

She calls Susie and Clara "Guck and Ben." We have dropped "Bay" and adopted "Ben," in consequence.

Jean is incomparably sweet, and good, and entertaining. Sits in my lap, at the fag-end of dinner, and eats "Jean quum" (crumbs,) and messes-up the table with "Jean shawt" (salt,) puts "Jean fum" (plums—i.e. grapes) in "Jean himble-bo" (finger-bowl) and says "Naughty George—ve'y naughty George," when George brushes off her salt. Won't consent that she is mamma's blessed Miss Jane—no, is "*Papa* besshy Mish Chain."

*

Ben had a birth-day party of 67 children, 8th of June, and at it Jean picked up scarlet fever and was a prisoner some weeks. It delayed our journey to Elmira by six weeks, and delayed "Life on the Mississippi" more than twice as long.

*

1882. Xmas. Eve.

Mamma brought home a variety of presents for distribution, and allowed Susie to see those that were to be sent to Patrick's family. Among these was an unusually handsome and valuable sled for Jimmy, on which a stag was painted, and also, in gilt letters the word "DEER." Susie was enthusiastic over everything until she came to this sled; then she became sober and silent. Yet this sled was the very thing she was expected to be most eloquent over, for it was the jewel of the lot. Mamma was surprised; also disappointed; and said, "Why Susie, doesn't it please you?—isn't it fine?"

Susie hesitated; plainly did not like to have to say the thing that was in her mind; but being pressed, she got it out—haltingly: "Well, mamma, it *is* fine, and of course it *did* cost a good deal—but—why should that be mentioned?" And seeing she was not understood, she pointed to that word "deer!" Poor thing, her heart was in the right place, but her orthography wasn't. However, she knows the difference between dear and deer now—and permanently.

*

Susie said to aunt Clara the immaculate conception was not puzzling to her.

*

1883 March and April.

During these months and part or all of February, Patrick's seven children had a rough time of it, with the dire scarlet fever. Two of them escaped very narrowly. Clara Spaulding arrived on a visit, and Susie gave her a full and animated account of these momentous and marvelous things. Aunt Clara said:

"Why, considering how very very low, those two were, it seems next to miraculous that they got well. But they *did* get well?"

"Yes—both of them." Then, after a pause—pensively: *"It was a great disappointment to us."*

Aunt Clara was astounded—in fact, pretty nearly paralyzed; but she didn't "let on"—only said—

"Why?"

"Well, you know, aunt Clara"—another pause—grave deliberation, to get her thought into form—"Well, you see, aunt Clara, we've never had any experience of a funeral."

"Oh, I see. But you—you didn't want the children to die?"

"Well, no—not that, exactly. But—in case they did die—well,—they—we—well, you know, we've never had a funeral."

"Still, it was scarlet fever, and you wouldn't have been allowed to attend it."

"No—I suppose Mamma wouldn't have let us. But then, you know, we could have observed it."

It was the eclat of the thing—the pomp, and solemnity and commotion. That is what Susie was after.

*

1883 May 1.

Good Memory. Two months ago I took Jean in the nursery bathroom, gave her a lecture about some bad behavior, and then spanked her. The result was disastrous. She went into a passion of furious and vindictive crying, mixed with yells for Rosa. I whipped her again, after vainly trying to get her to say "Please." Her constant reply was "I won't—Jean won't." I whipped her a third time—between spats reiterating gently and kindly, "Only say *please*—that is all—then Jean can go to Rosa." She merely continued to howl, and call for Rosa, and say "I *won't!*" Most fortunately mamma came in and proposed to continue the thing and give me a rest. I was mighty glad to get out of the dilemma—and was resolved to not get into another like it soon. Of course mamma, with her superior tact, soon got out of Jean all that was wanted.

I naturally supposed that my effort had gone for nothing. But not so. A full month later, Rosa heard a mouse gnawing, in the nursery one midnight, and said "Shoo!" Jean sat up in her crib and said—

"Better go way, mousie—papa come, take you in bath woom and spat you and make you say *pease*."

And last night she suggested that Rosa had been naughty about something, and wanted me to take her in the bath-room and spank her and make her say "pease."

*

1883 June 8 Clara's birthday—aged 9.

Clara picked up a book—"Daniel Boone, by John S. C. Abbott" and found on the fly-leaf a comment of mine, in pencil; puzzled over it, couldn't quite make it out; her mother took it and read it to her, as follows: "A poor slovenly book; a mess of sappy drivel and bad grammar." Clara said, with entire seriousness (not comprehending the meaning but charmed with the sound of the words,) "O, that must be lovely!" and carried the book away and buried herself in it.

*

1883 Summer at the Farm.

Poor Jean, now three years old, has been neglected in this record. But it is largely her own fault, she having been chary of making reportable speeches.

The other day she asked if she might go and swing herself in "the big swing." Mamma denied the petition, and suggested that Jean was too small. Jean responded, "I can if I *could*, mamma." (Meaning, I *can* swing myself, if I could get permission.)

Jean in 1884, aged three.

*

Toward Xmas. Hartford.

OBITUARY.

Death of Hon. Jacob Burrough of Cape Girardeau.

Special to the Republican.

CAPE GIRARDEAU, Mo., Dec. 3.—Hon. Jacob H. Burrough, an old and prominent citizen, died of paralysis last night in this city in the fifty-eighth year of his age. Judge Burrough had been in failing health for about a year and, while on a visit to Minneapolis last summer for his health, had a stroke of paralysis which hastened his return to his home. On last Friday night he experienced a second stroke which terminated fatally.

He had filled numerous offices of honor and trust. Prominent among them were those of probate judge, regent of the S.E. Normal school and city auditor. He leaves a wife and three grown children who have the sincere sympathy of the whole community. The funeral services will take place to-morrow and will be conducted by Rev. J. W. Rosenborough of the Presbyterian church. The remains will be interred in Larimer cemetery.

I stepped into the nursery on my way to the billiard room after breakfast. I had a newspaper-cutting in my hand, just received in the mail, and its spirit was upon me—the spirit of funerals and gloom. Jean sat playing on the floor, the incandescent core of a conflagration of flooding sunlight—and she and her sunny splendors were suggestive of just the opposite spirit. She said, with great interest,—

"What is it in the little piece of paper you got in yo' hand, papa—what do it say?"

I said, impressively, and meaning to impress *her*, —

"It tells about an old, old friend of mine, Jean—friend away back yonder years and years and years ago, when I was young—very dear friend, and now he is dead, Jean."

She uttered an ejaculation and I a response.

Then she looked earnestly up from down there, and said, —

"Is he gone up in heaven, papa?"

"Yes," I said, "he is gone up in heaven."

A reflective pause—then she said, —

"Was he down on the earth, papa—down here?"

"Yes, he was down here on the earth, where we are."

She lowered her face, now grown very grave, and reflected again, two or three moments. Then she lifted it quickly to mine, and inquired with a burning interest, —

"And did along comed a blackbird and nipped off his nose?"

The solemnity of the occasion was gone to the devil in a moment—as far as I was concerned; though Jean was not aware that *she* had done anything toward that result. She was asking simply and solely for information, and was not intending to be lightsome or frivolous.

*

May, '84

A heavy wagon went by, outside—we all questioned what the noise might be. Jean said, "I hear it thunder, and that's Elisa." (German nurse.)

*

Mention was made of a certain young lady, at breakfast; and Susie remarked that she was very pretty. Her mother said no, she had a good face, a face which answered to her exceptionally fine character, but she would hardly call it a pretty face. Susie said—

"But mama, I think that when a person has a good figure and a pleasant face that one likes to look at, she *is* pretty."

Rev. Thos. K. Beecher was present, and said it was a nice distinction, and that Susie's position was sound.

*

Following out a suggestion made by Mrs. Henry J. Brooks, we established the rule that each member of the household must come to table armed with a fact. Susie's first fact was in substance as follows:

Two great exiles and former opponents in the field, met in Ephesus, Hannibal and Scipio. Scipio asked Hannibal whom he considered the greatest general the world had produced.

"Alexander"—and he explained why.

"And who was the next greatest?"

"Pyrrhus"—and he explained why.

"But where do you place yourself then?"

"If I had conquered you, I would place myself before the others."

And Susie's comment was:

"That attracted me, it was just like papa—he is so frank about his books." (So frank in praising them.)

*

Apl. 4 1885.

[General Grant is still living, this morning.]

*

Susie: "I think it is pitiful, mamma's faith in Jean's ability to keep a secret." [At breakfast, this—the mamma thus discussed and brought under criticism, sick and upstairs abed. I carried it straight up. Great fun.]

[Jean keeps part of a secret, but always lets the other part—the important part—out.]

*

Apl. 4 1885. Susie 13

Susie began writing a biography of me ten or fifteen days ago; the dearest compliment I could imagine, and the most gratifying.

*

June 1885.

Susie thoughtfully: "How one happiness gets in the way of another, and one cannot have them both!" "What is it, now?" "Well, I am to go to Cousin Susie Warner's in the morning, and now I have been to the kitchen and it turns out that we are going to have Miss Corey and fish balls for breakfast." [The collocation is the point—if you don't perceive it yourself.]

*

June 7th.

Jean: "I wonder God lets us have so much ducks—Patrick kills them so."

*

Sept. '84.

Old Clark, the low-down, the intemperate, used to go by the farm, last month, swearing. Susie's excuse for him (to Miss Foote) was, "he can't help it, he doesn't know any *nice intellectual naughty words.*" [From which the necessary inference is that she moves in a circle which does.]

~~~

MARK TWAIN

At the Farm

Summer of 1884—Jean nearly 4 yrs old.

She goes out to the barn with one of us every evening toward 6 o'clock, to look at the cows—which she adores—no weaker word can express her feeling for them. She sits rapt and contented while David milks the three, making a remark now and then—always about the cows. The time passes slow and drearily for her attendant, but not for her—she could stand a week of it. When the milking is finished and "Blanche," "Jean" and "the cross cow" turned into the adjoining little cow-lot, we have to set Jean on a shed in that lot, and stay by her half an hour till Elisa the German nurse comes to take her to bed. The cows merely stand there, amongst the ordure, which is dry or sloppy according to the weather, and do nothing—yet the mere sight of them is all-sufficient for Jean; she requires nothing more. The other evening, after contemplating them a long time, as they stood in the muddy muck chewing the cud, she said with deep and reverent appreciation—

"Ain't this a sweet little garden!"

*

Susie (aged 12) came to her mother a week or two ago with a weight on her conscience. But she found it hard to begin her confession, her crime was of such an unworthy sort. Finally, under encouragement, she got a start, and said—

"Well, mama, you know Jervis and Julia are always talking about uncle Charley as if he was just everything—as if nobody in the world was so great and remarkable as he is. I'm *proud* of papa, and I can't bear it to have them always talking that way about uncle Charley: why it's just as if he was papa's *equal.* Well, this afternoon Jervis—what do you reckon he asked me? He asked me what *Manuscript* was. I told him, and then—well, mama, I *couldn't* help it,—I said that if his papa was an *author,* he wouldn't have to ask that question. I was ashamed, right away, but you know it was too late, mama."

[However, she seemed to find some faint little grain of comfort in the fact, that deadly as the shot was, it had apparently gone through Jervis without his being aware that he had been hit.]

*

During an interchange of severe criticisms of the dog Flash's manners and conduct, Susie said—

"Mama, if you loved that dog as you do your children, he would act right enough."

[That is to say, she would train him, with a strict and affectionate hand. A very good compliment.]

*

Mother came up 4th of July night and took Jean's room, and *she* was transferred to another. Next morning Jean blackguarded that new room to me, eloquently and without stint; but in aunt Sue's presence not a word of criticism concerning it could be wrung from her by any trick or art. It was considered that she showed a fine and delicate feeling in the matter.

*

July 7, 1884. Yesterday evening our cows (after being inspected and worshiped by Jean from the shed for an hour,) wandered off down into the pasture, and left her bereft. I thought I was going to get back home, now, but that was an error. Jean knew of some more cows, in a field somewhere, and took my hand and led me thitherward. When we turned the corner and took the right-hand road, I saw that we should presently be out of range of call and sight; so I began to argue against continuing the expedition, and

Jean began to argue in favor of it—she using English for light skirmishing, and German for "business." I kept up my end with vigor, and demolished her arguments in detail, one after the other, till I judged I had her about cornered. She hesitated a moment, then answered up sharply:

"Wir werden kein mehr darüber sprechen!" [We won't talk any more about it.]

It nearly took my breath away; though I thought I might possibly have misunderstood. I said:

"Why, you little rascal! Was hast du gesagt?"

But she said the same words over again, and in the same decided way. I suppose I ought to have been outraged; but I wasn't, I was charmed. And I suppose I ought to have spanked her; but I didn't, I fraternized with the enemy, and we went on and spent half an hour with the cows.

*

Mama was speaking of a servant who had been pretty unveracious, but was now "trying to tell the truth." Susie was a good deal surprised, and said she shouldn't think anybody would have to *try* to tell the truth.

~~~

Quarry Farm Diary

June 28th Quarry Farm—Elmira N.Y.

On June 19th we arrived in Elmira, we went directly to Mothers spending a little more than a week with her. The six grand children had a delightful time together, and we elders all had a good visit. Yesterday morning we left Mothers and two loads of us drove up here, Charley bringing Ida, little Ida, Julia, Mr Clemens and me. The other load being Susy, Clara, Jervis, Elize (the nurse) and Jean. The load of children reached the farm first. At once after the second arrival the children all went out to see a new donkey that had been purchased in Kansas and sent to the farm for them. Jean's first exclamation was "dear old fellow" as she advanced toward the "creature" with a little imbarassed air. The children all had a ride on the donken then Charley and Ida started down the hill with their little flock—and we began to get ourselves settled for our Summer's stay here. Susy said "how good Aunt Sue is to let us come here and stay all Summer." I most heartily echo that sentiment. The great interest with the children during these two days since we came has been the donkey. She seems a docile beast, the children have caught her in the field, bridled her and mounted her alone, but when they would ride their father went with them. We hope the donkey has no bad tricks that will in any way frighten or inconvenience the children. They have named her Patience Cadichon, pronouncing it, Kaditchin.

This morning Theodore, Sue, Susy and I went down to church, it was Anniversary Sunday, there was a very large number baptised, first infants, later in the service young people, and older people all excepting the infants professed their faith. It was an exceedingly interesting and touching service.

[. . .]

July 2nd

Jean has commenced now regularly her lessons every day, that is learning to read. Every morning she comes into the dining room as we are about through breakfast, and says "I don't want a German lesson this morning, need I?" I say "oh yes"—we go into the bay window, sit on the sofa in the beloved "Farm" parlor and have a lesson, the plan is to have a half hour lesson but Jean is so interested after she has put in her one protest, that she always desires a longer lesson than the appointed time. Today Jean achieved a moral victory over herself. The older children had to go to the dentist I went with them—When Jean knew we were all to go she desired very much to go too, but when she was told she could not she gave it up very uncomplainingly. As we were seated in the carriage she came running and saying "I 'ant (want) to kiss you goo' bye Mamma"—she was lifted up for the kiss and she kept saying "goo' bye Mamma"—her little lips trembling, she did not like to be left behind, but she did not allow the tears to come. I hated to leave the dear little face so but I was compelled to.

Susy is reading aloud to me Schillers "Yungfrau von Orleans"—she reads it very well and it is delightful to read it with her. Tonight I was reading to Susy and Clara from a book "Life and her Children" a very interesting book on the lower forms of Animal Life. I came to something about Carbonic Acid—and as we spoke a little about it Clara said, I always like to talk aloud to myself when I am alone in the woods, because I like to give the trees Carbonic Acid. The blessed child it was so sweetly and innocently said.

July 12th

[. . .] Susy is reading Scott's "Betrothal," tonight she said to me Scott has a cool way of writing—even when the event is exciting he writes of it

Clara with her calf Jumbo, 1884.

coolly. Today as we were reading in the Bible together I took Clara's Bible
from her to look at something and a poor uneven little piece of paper fell
out, written closely on both sides, I saw at a glance that it was of interest
to me, that some of the childs thoughts were on it, she picked it up and
evidently did not want it seen—but I insisted until she gave it to me—Susy
saying too "Why Clara it is real sweet I saw it in your Bible the other day."
I read it and later when Clara stepped out of the room Susy said "that little

piece of paper made me know Clara better than I ever did before" This is what was on the paper—exactly except that I can not copy the dear little irregularities of the childish hand.

"Be good to Susy, be not rude, overbearing, cross or pick her up, Be considerate of Eliza (the nurse), and put yourself in her place. Be as sweet and generous to Jean as Susy is and even more so, and be not selfish with the donkey but think how much you like to ride her and Jean enjoys it just about as much. Be sweet to Mamma and when you see that she is tired you ought to ask her as few questions as you can not to bother her. Be not cross and unmannerly to Julie even if you do think her queer, perhaps she thinks you queer. Be good always"

There were places where she was troubled with the 3rd person form, would at first use the 1st person and then write over it. It is a precious little document and I wish that I could keep it but evidently it is a help to the child she asked for it tonight, I told her I would give it to her tomorrow, but I do hate to have it lost. It has to me a real à Kempis ring about it.

[. . .]

July 26th

Jean birthday. Soon after a nine o'clock breakfast we made ready Jean's table of gifts in the parlor—we had it in the parlor instead of the little arbor where we have generally had it because Clara has a sore throat and it did not seem best for her to go to the arbor as it was windy. The dear little five-year-old maiden had a very happy time, with her various little articles. The only article of any value was a heavy silver spoon from Mother, but she had a number of little playthings that interested her. Her father was in New York, he telegraphed her wishing her sixty five returns, where shall we all be at that time. 1950. Jean saw the little birds picking up seeds and worms at all sorts of irregular times and she said to Aunt Sue "doesn't it hurt the birds to eat between meals."

[. . .]

Sept 8th 1885

I began yesterday to show Jean something about insects—we went out and got a grasshopper, but it jumped about so in the glass where we put it that she could not see it very well. I did not want her to kill it, because I cannot get away from the feeling that it must greatly blunt a childs sensitivity to allow it to kill the little creatures. We were able to examine a lady bug after a fashion without hurting it. Last night I got one or two insects that killed themselves in the light of the lamp. Today I was showing her their different parts—she said she had a dead fly up in her room, so she brought it to me. I told her we would find what dead insects we could today and examine them tomorrow.

While we were eating our dinner, Jean came into the dining room, came up to my side and laid down on the table cloth by the side of my plate a handful of dead flies—saying triumphantly, "Mamma I found all those dead creatures in the kitchen" Of course there was nothing to do but praise the dear little midge for her success in finding "dead creatures," but one would have prefered to have her keep them until one had finished eating. However I put them on a plate and told her to take them into the parlor, She started but at the door met the cat Sour Mash, and as Sour Mash was very anxious to have the contents of the plate, Jean gave her the flies saying "Mamma Sour Mash wants them so much I think she can have them and I can get more." However she ow[n]ed afterward that she did not know where she could get any more, because she had gotten all there were in the kitchen.

Sept 14th

We start for New York tomorrow the 15th leaving this beloved Quarry Farm. We expect to spend a few days in New York and then on to Hartford.

This afternoon as I lay on the bed feeling rather depressed at the thought of leaving Mother and Sue and the friends here and a little tired from the packing &c Susy came to my bed side bringing a little bag that she had filled with articles to amuse Jean on the journey. It was delightful to see the arrangements that she had made—there were paper dolls cut out ready for Jean to make the faces on them, a piece of silk with a needle and pieces of thread for her to sew—a crochet neadle with worsted for her to "heckel," buttons for her to sew on, a paper book which Susy had made for her, cutting out pictures and pasting them in the book, then writing storries about them—all this and more to amuse Jean on the journey to New York tomorrow. While I lay on the bed mourning she was doing something for the pleasure of some one else, the blessed child. Probably the next time I write in this book will be in Hartford, if we are spared to arrive there safely.

~~~

Mark Twain by Susy Clemens

We are a very happy family! we consist of papa, mamma, Jean Clara and me. It is papa I am writing about, and I shall have no trouble in not knowing what to say about him, as he is a very striking character. Papa's appearance has been discribed many times, but very incorectly; he has beautiful curly grey hair, not any too thick, or any too long, just right; A roman nose, which greatly improves the beauty of his features, kind blue eyes, and a small mustache, he has a wonderfully shaped head, and profile, he has a very good figure in short he is an extrodinarily fine looking man. All his features are perfect exept that he hasn't extrodinary teeth. His complexion is very fair, and he doesn't ware a beard.

He is a very good man, and a very funny one; he <u>has</u> got a temper but we all of us have in this family. He is the loveliest man I ever saw, or ever hope to see; and oh so absent minded! He does tell perfectly delightful stories, Clara and I used to sit on each arm of his chair, and listen while he told us stories about the pictures on the wall.

His favorite game is billiards, and when he is tired, and wishes to rest himself he stays up all night and plays billiards, it seems to rest his head. He smokes a great deal almost incessantly. He has the mind of an author exactly, some of the simplest things he cant understand. Our burglar alarm is often out of order, and papa had been obliged to take the mahogany room off from the alarm altogether for a time, because the burglar alarm had been in the habit of ringing even when the mahogany room window was closed. At length he thought that perhaps the burglar alarm might be in order, and he decided to try and see; accordingly he put it on, and then went down and opened the window; consequently the alarm bell rang,

it would even if the alarm had been in order. Papa went despairingly up stairs, and said to mamma, "Livy the mahogany room wont go on, I have just opened the window to see." "Why Youth" mamma replied, "if you've opened the window why of coarse the alarm will ring!' "That's what I've opened it for, why I just went down to see if it would ring"! Mamma tried to explain to papa that when he wanted to go and see whether the alarm would ring while the window was closed, he mustn't go and open the window. But in vain, papa couldn't understand, and got very impatient with mamma for trying to make him believe an impossible thing true.

He has a peculiar gait we like, it seems just to sute him, but most people do not; he always walks up and down the room while thinking and between each coarse at meals. He is very fond of animals particularly of cats, we had a dear little grey kitten once, that he named "Lazy" (papa always wares grey to match his hair and eyes) and he would carry him around on his shoulder, it was a mighty pretty sight! the grey cat sound asleep against papa's grey coat and hair. The names that he has given our different cats, are realy remarkably funny, they are namely "Stray Kit," "Abner" "Motly," "Freulein," "Lazy" "Bufalo Bill" and "Soapy Sall" "Cleveland," "Sour Mash" and "Famine"

Papa uses very strong language, but I have an idea not nearly so strong as when he first married mamma. A lady acquaintance of his is rather apt to interupt what one is saying, and papa told mamma that he thought he should say to the lady's husband "I am glad Mrs. _____ wasn't present when the Deity said '"let ther be light"'

Papapa said the other day, "I am a mugwump and a mugwump is pure from the marrow out." (Papa knows that I am writing this biography of him, and he said this for it.) He doesn't like to go to church at all, why I never understood, until just now, he told us the other day, that he couldn't bear to hear any one talk but himself, but that he could listen to himself talk for hours without getting tired, of course he said this in joke, but I've no dought it was founded on truth. One of his latest books was the "Prince and the Pauper," and it is unquestionably the best book he has ever written, some people want him to keep to his old style, some gentelman wrote him, "I enjoyed "Huckelberry Finn" immensly and am glad to see that you have returned to your old style." ***** That enoyed me greatly, because it trobles me to have so few people know papa, I mean realy know him, they think of Mark Twain as a humorist joking at every thing; "and with a mop of reddish brown hair, which sorely needs the barbar's brush, a roman nose, short stubby mustache, a sad care-worn face, with many crow's feet," &c. that is the way people picture papa, I have wanted papa to write a book that would reveal something of his kind sympathetic nature, and the "Prince and Pauper" partly does it. The book is full of lovely charming ideas, and oh the language! it is perfect, I think. I think that one of the most touching scenes in it, is where the pauper is riding on horsback with his nobles in the recognition procession, and he sees his mother, oh and then what followed; how she runs to his side, when she sees him throw up his hand palm outward, and is rudely pushed off by one [of] the king's officers. And then how the little pauper's consience troubles him as he rembers the shameful words that were falling from his lips, when she was torn from his side. "I know you not woman" And how his grandeurs were stricken valueless, and his pride consumed to ashes. It is a wonderfully beautiful and touching little scene, and papa has described it so wonderfully. I never saw a man with so much variety of feeling as papa has; now the "Prince and the Pauper" is full of touching places, but there is most always a streak of humor in them somewhere   now in the "Coronation"—in the stirring coronation, just after the little king has got his crown back again papa brings that in about the seal, where the Pauper says he used the seal "to crack nuts with," oh it is so funny and nice! papa very seldom writes a passage without some humorisam in it some where, and I dont think he ever will.

Papa was born in Misouri, his mother is Grandma Clemens (Jane Lampton Clemens,) of Kentucky, Grandpa Clemens was of the F.F.V's of Virginia. Clara and I are sure that papa played the trick on Grandma, about the whipping, that is related in "The Adventures of Tom Sayer" "Hand me that switch." The switch hovered in the air the peril was desperate,—"My, look behind you aunt,"! The old lady whirled round and snatched her skirts out of danger. The lad fled on the instant, scrambled up the high board fence, and dissapeared over it."' And we know papa played "Hookey" all the time. and how readily would papa have pretended to be dying so as not to have to go to school!

Grandma couldn't make papa go to school, so she let him go into a printing office to learn the trade. He did so, and gradually picked up enough education to enable him to do about as well as those who were more studious in early life. He was about 20 years old when he went on the Mississippi as a pilot. Just befor he started on his tripp Mrs. Clemens asked him to promise her on the Bible not to touch intoxicating liquors or swear, and he said "Yes mother I will," and he kept that promise seven years, when Grandma released him from it. After papa had been a pilot on the Mississippi, for a time, Uncle Orion Clemens, was appointed secretary of the State of Nevada, and papa went with him out to Nevada to be his secratary. Afterwards he became interested in mining in California, the[n] he reported for a newspaper, and was on several newspapers; then he was sent to the Sandwich islands to   After that he came back to America and his friends wanted him to lecture, so he lectured; then he went to Philidelphia, and found a situation in a printing office; Then he went abroad on "the Quaker City," and on board that ship he became equainted with Uncle Charlie, Mr. C. J. Langdon of New York, papa and uncle Charlie soon became friends, and when they returned from their journey, Grandpa Langdon, unc[l]e Charlie's father, told uncle Charlie to invite Mr. Clemens to dine with them at the St Nicholas hotel N.Y.   Papa accepted the invitation, and went to dine at the "St Nicholas" with Grand-papa, and there he met mamma, Olivia Louise Langdon, first. But they did not meet again until the next August; because papa went away to California, and there wrote the "Inocense Abroad."

Mamma was the daughter of Mr. Jervis Langdon, (I don't know whether Grandpa had a middle name or not) and Mrs. Olivia Lewis Langdon, of

Elmira New York. She had one brother, and one sister, uncle Charlie, Charles J. Langdon; and aunt Susie, Susan Langdon. Mamma loved Grand-papa more than any one else in all the world, he was her idol, and she his, I think mamma's love for Grandpa must have very much resembled, my love for mamma. Grandpa was a great and good man, and we all think of him with respect, and love. Mamma was an invalid when she was young, and had to give up study a long time.

Soon papa [came] back east, and papa and mamma were married. Papa wrote mamma a great many beautiful love letters when he was engaged to mamma, but mamma says I am too young to see them yet; I asked papa what I should do for I didn't [know] how I could write a Biography of him without his love-letters, papa said that I could write mamma's oppinion of them, and that would do just as well. So I will do as papa says, and mamma says she thinks they are the loveliest love-letters that ever were written, she says she thinks that Hawthorne's love-letters to Mrs. Hawthorne are far inferior to these. Mamma [and papa] were going to board first in Bufalo and Grandpa said he would find them a good boarding house. But he afterwards told mamma that he had bought a pretty house for them, and had it all beautifully furnished, he had also hired a young coachman, and had bought a horse for them, which all would be ready waiting for them, when they should arive in Bufalo; but he wanted to keep it a secret, from "Youth" as Grandpa called papa. What a delightful surprise it was! Grandpa went down to Bufalo with mamma and papa. And when they drove up to the house, papa said he thought, the landlord of such a boarding house, must charge a great deal, to those who wanted to live there. And when the secret was told papa was delighted beyond all degree. Mamma has told me the story many times, and I asked her what papa said, when Grandpa told him that the delightful boarding house was his home, mamma answered that he was rather embariesed, and so delighted he didn't know what to say. About 6 months after papa and mamma were married Grandpapa died; it was a terrible blow on mamma, and papa told aunt Sue he thought Livy would never smile again she was so broken hearted. Mamma couldn't have had a greater sorrow than that of dear Grandpapa's death, or any that could equal it exept the death of papa. Mamma helped take care of Grandpapa during his illness, and she couldn't give up hope till the end had realy come. After that she went back to Bufalo; and a few months after dear little Langdon was born. Mamma named him Langdon after Grandpapa, he was a wonderfully beautiful little boy, but very, very delicate. He had wonderful blue eyes, but such a blue that mamma has never been able to discribe them to me, so that I could see them clearly in my mind's eye. His delicate health was a constant anxiety to mamma, and he was so good and sweet, that that must have troubled her too, as I know it did. While a little baby he used to carry a pencil in his little hand, that was his great plaything; I believe he was very seldom seen without one in his hand. When he was in aunt Susy's arms and would want to go to mamma he would hold out his hands to her with the backs of his hands out toward her, instead of with his palmes out. About a year after Langdon was born, I was born, and my chief occupation then was to cry so I must have added greatly to mamma's care! Soon after little Langdon was born, papa and mamma moved to Hartford to live. Their house in Bufalo reminded them too much of dear Grandpapa, so they moved to Hartford soon after he died. Soon after little Langdon was born a friend of mamma's came to visit her (Emma Nigh.) And she was taken with the typhoid fever, while visiting mamma. At length she became so delirious, and was so hard to take care of, that mamma had to send to some of her friends in Elmira N.Y. to come and help take care of her. Aunt Clara, came, (Miss Clara L. Spaulding) she is no relation of ours but we call her aunt Clara, because she is such a great friend of mamma's. She came and helped mamma take care of Ema Nigh, but in spite of all the good care that she received, she grew worse and died. Just after I mentioned, that mamma and papa couldn't stay in their house in Bufalo because it reminded so much of Grandpapa, mamma received a letter from aunt Susy, in which aunt Susy says a good deal about Grandpapa, and the letter shows so clearly how much every one that knew Grandpapa

Langdon Clemens, 1871.

loved and respected him; that mamma let me take it to copy what is in it about Grandpapa. And mamma thought it would fit in nicely here.

The Farm   April 16th/85.

"Livy dear,

Are you not reminded by todays report of Gen. Grant of father? You remember how as Judge Smith and others whom father had chosen as executors were going out of the room, he said "Gentlemen I shall live to bury you all," smiled and was cheerful. At that time he had far less strength than Gen. Grant seems to have, but that same wonderful courage to battle with the foe. All along, there has been much to remind me of father, of his quiet patience—in Gen. Grant. There certainly is a marked likeness in the souls of the two men. Watching day by day the reports from the nations sick room brings to mind so vividly the days of that summer of 1870. And yet they seem so far away, I seemed as a child compared with now, both in years and experiance. The best and the hardest of life have been since then, to me, and I know this [is] so in your life. All before seems dreamy—I supose this [is] because our lives had to be all readjusted to go on without that great power in them. Father was quietly such a power in so many lives beside ours Livy dear,—not in kind or degree the same to any one, but oh a power! the evening of the last company, I was so struck with the fact, when Mr. Atwater stood quietly before fathers portrait a long time, and turning to me said, "we shall never see his like again"—with a tremble and a choking in his voice,—this after 15 yrs. and from a business friend. And some stranger a week ago spoke of his habit of giving as so remarkable, he having heard of father's generosity." ✱✱✱✱✱✱✱✱✱✱✱✱✱✱

Papa made arangements to read at Vassar College the 1st of May, and I went with him. We went by way of N.Y. City; mamma went with us to New York and stayed two days, to do some shopping. We started Tuesday at ½ past two o'clock in the after noon, and reached New York about ¼ past 6.

Papa went right up to Gen. Grants from the station, and mamma, and I went to the Everett House. Aunt Clara came to supper with us up in our room. We were going to the theater right after supper, and we expected papa to take us there, and to come home as early as he could. But we got through dinner, and he didn't come, and didn't come, and mamma got more perplexed and worried, but at [last] we thought we would have to go without him, so we put on our things, and started down stairs but before we'd goten half down, we met papa coming up, with a great bunch of roses in his hand, he explained that the reason he was so late was that his watch stopped, and he didn't notice, and kept thinking it, an hour earlier than it realy was. The roses he carried were some Col. Grant sent to mamma. We went to the theater and enjoyed "Adonis," the play acted very much, we reached home about ½ past 11 o'clock, and went right to bed. Wed. morning we got up rather late, and had breakfast about ½ past 9 o'clock. After breakfast mamma went out shopping, and papa and I went to see papa's agent about some busniess matters. After papa had gotten through talking to Cousin Charlie, his agent, we went to get a friend of papa's (Major Pond) to go and see a dog show with us. Then we went to see the dogs with Major Pond and we had a delightful time seeing so many dogs together; when we got through seeing the dogs, papa thought he would go up and see Gen. Grant, and I went with him,—this was April 29th 1885. Papa went up into Gen. Grant's room, and he took me with him, I felt greatly honored and delighted when papa took me into Gen. Grant's room and let me see the Gen. and Col. Grant; for Gen Grant is a man I shall be glad all my life that I have seen. Papa and Gen. Grant had a long talk together; and papa has writen an account of his talk and visit with Gen. Grant for me to put into this Biography.

1885.

"April 29th 1885. "I called on Gen. Grant and took Susie with me. The Gen. was looking and feeling far better, than he had looked or felt for some months. He had ventured to work again on his book that morning—the first time he had done any work for perhaps a month. This morning's work was his first attempt at dictating and it was a thourough success to his great delight. He had always said that it would be impossible for him to dictate anything; but I had said that he was noted for cleanness of statement, and a narative was simply a statement of consecutive facts, and that he was consequently peculiarly qualified and equipped for dictation. This turned out to be true; for he had dictated two hours that morning to a short hand writer, had never hessitated for words, had not repeated himself, and the manuscript, when finished needed no revision. The two hours work was an account of Appomatox, and this was such an extremely important feature, that his book would necessarily have been severely lame without it. Therefore I had taken a short hand writer there before to see if I could not get him to write at least a few lines about Appomatox; but he was at that time, not well enough to undertake it. I was aware that of all the hundred versions of Appomatox, not one was realy corect   Therefore I was extremely anxious that he should leave behind him the truth. His throat was not disstressing him and his voice was much better and stronger than usual. He was so delighted to have got Appomatox, accomplished, once more in his life—to have got the matter off his mind—that he was as talkative as his old self. He received Susy very pleasantly, and then fell to talking about certain matters which he hoped to be able to dictate next day; and he said in substance, that— among other things—he wanted to settle once for all a question that had been bandied about from mouth to mouth and from newspaper to newspaper and that question was: with whom orriginated the idea of the march to the sea,—was it Grant's or was it Sherman's idea?

Whether I or some one else—being anxious to get the important fact settled—asked him with whom the idea orriginated, I dont remember. But I remember his answer; I shall always remember his answer.

Gen Grant said. "Neither of us originated the idea of Shermans march to the sea. The enemy did it."

He went on to say that the enemy very necessarily orriginates a great many of the plans that the general on the opposite side gets the credit for; at the same time the enemy is doing that, he is laying open other moves, which the General sees and takes advantage of.

In this case Sherman had a plan all thought out of course. He meant to destroy the two remaining railroads in that part of the country and that would have finnished up that region. But Gen. How did not play the military part that he was expected to play. On the contrary Gen. How made a dive at Chattanooga. This left the march to the sea open to Sherman. And so after sending part of his army [t]o defend and hold what he had conquered in the Chattanooga region, he was perfectly free to proceed with the rest of it through Georgia. He saw the opportunity and he would not have been fit for his place, if he had not seized it.

"He wrote me, (the Gen. is speaking) what his plan was, and I sent him word to go ahead. My staff were opposed to the movement," (I think he said it tried to persuade him to stop Sherman.) The [chief] of his staff the Gen. said even went so far, as to go to Washington without the General's knowledge, and get the ear of the authaurities, and he succeded in erasing their fears to such an extent that they telegraphed me to stop Sherman. Out of deferance to the goverment I telegraphed Sherman and stopped him twenty four hours; and then considering that that was deferance enough to the government, I telegraphed him to go ahead again."

I have not tried to give the Generals language but only the general idea of what he said.

The thing that mainly struck me was his terse remark that the enemy orriginated the idea of the march to the sea.

It struck me because it was so suggestive of the generals epe-gramatic fashion,—saying a great deal, in a single crisp sentence."

Mark Twain.

After papa and Gen. Grant had, had their talk, we went back to the hotel where mamma was, and papa told mamma all about his interview with Gen. Grant. Mamma and I had a nice quiet afternoon together; and papa went to read in public; there were a great many authors that read that Thursday afternoon beside papa; I would have liked to have gone and heard papa read, but papa said he was going to read in Vasser just what he was planning to read in New York. So I staid at home with mamma. The next day mamma planned to take the four o'clock car back to Hartford. We rose quite early that morning and went to the "Vienna Bakery" and took breakfast there. From there we went to a German book store, and bought some German books for Clara's birth day. Then mamma and I went to do some shopping, and papa went to see Gen. Grant. After we had finnished doing our shopping, we went home to the hotel together. When we entered our rooms in the hotel, we saw on the table a vase full of exquisett red roses. Mamma who is very fond of flowers, exclaimed, "Oh I wonder who could have sent them"? We both looked at the card in the midst of the roses, and saw that it was written on in papa's hand writing, it was written in German, "Liebes Geschenk on die Mamma." Mamma was delighted. Papa came home, and gave mamma her ticket; and after visiting a while with her, went to see Maj. Pond, and mamma and I sat down to our lunch. After lunch most of our time was taken up with packing. And at about 3 o'clock, we went to escort mamma to the train. We got on board the train with her, and stayed with her about 5 minutes; and then we said good bye to her and the train started for Hartford. It was the first time I had ever beene away from home without Mamma in my life, although I was 13 yrs. old. Papa and I rode back to the hotel, and got Maj. Pond, and then went to see the "Brooklyn Bridge" we went across it to Brooklyn on the cars, and then walked back across it from Brooklyn to New York. We enjoyed looking at the beautiful scenery, and we could see the bridge moove under the intense heat of the sun. We had a perfectly delightful time, but wer pretty tired when we got back to the hotel.

Maj. Pond, and Miss Jessie, a friend of his took dinner with us up in our hotel rooms. They left a little while, after we had finnished dinner and then papa and I went to bed. The next morning we rose early, took our breakfast and took an early train to Poughkeepsie. We had a very pleasant journey to Poughkeepsie, the Hudson, was magnificent shrouded with beautiful mists. When we arived at Poughkeepsie, it was raining quite hard; which fact greatly dissapointed me, because I very much wanted to see the outside buildings of Vassar College, and as it rained, that would be impossible. It was quite a long drive from the station to Vassar College, and papa and I had a nice long time to discuss and laugh over German profanity. One of the German phrases papa particularly enjoys, is "Ah heilige Maria, Mutter Jesus"! Jean has a german nurse and this was one of her phrases, there was a time when Jean exclaimed "Ach Gott!" to every trifle, but when mamma found it out, she was shocked and instantly put a stop to it.

We at, length reached Vassar College, and she looked very finely, her buildings and her grounds being very beautiful. We went to the front doore and rang the bell, the young girl who came to the doore wished to know who we wanted to see. Evidently we were not expected. Papa told her who we wanted to see, and she showed us to the parlor. We waited no one came; and waited no one came, still no one came, it was beginning to seem pretty awkward, "Well this is a pretty piece of business" papa exclaimed. At length we heard footsteps coming down the long corridors, and Miss C.——. (the lady who had invited papa) came into the room. She greeted papa very pleasantly, and they had a nice little chatt together. Soon the lady Principal also entered the room, and she was very pleasant and agreable. She showed us to our rooms, and said she would send for us when dinner was ready. We went into our rooms, but we had nothing to do for half an hour, exept to watch the rain drops as they fell upon the window panes. At last we were called to dinner and I went down without papa as he never eats anything in the middle of the day. I sat at the table with the lady Principal and enjoyed very much seing all the young girls trooping into the dining room. After dinner I went around the College with the young ladies and papa stayed in his room and smoked. When it was supper time papa went down and ate supper with us and we had a very delightful supper. After supper the young ladies went to their rooms to dress for the evening, papa went to his room and I went with the Lady Principal. At length the guests began to arive, but papa still remained in his room, until called for. Papa read in the chapell. It was the first time I had ever hurd him read in my life, that is in public. When he came out onto the stage I remember the people ₁b₁ehind me exclaimed "oh how queer he is! "isn't he funny!" I thought papa was very funny although I did not think him queer. He read "A Trying Situation" and "The Golden Arm" a ghost ₁story₁ that he heard dow₁n₁ South when he was a little boy. The Golden Arm papa had told me before but he had startelled me so that I did not much wish to hear it again. But I had resolved this time to ₁be₁ prepared and not to let myself be startled. But still papa did and very, very much, he startled the whole room full of people and they ₁jumped₁ as one man. The other story was also very funny and interesting and I enjoyed the ₁reading₁ inexpressibly much. After papa had finnished reading, we all went down to the Collation in the dining-room. And after that there was dancing and singing then the guests went away. And papa and I went to bed. The next morning we rose early took an early train for Hartford and reached Hartford at ½ past 2 o'clock. We were very glad to get back. *****

I stopped in the middle of mamma's early history to tell about our tripp to Vassar because I was afraid I would forget about it, now I will go on where I left off. Some time after Miss E. Nigh died Papa took mamma and little Langdon to Elmira for the summer. When in Elmira Langdon began to fail but I think mamma did not know just what was the matter with him. At last it was time for Papa to return to Hartford and Langdon was real sick at that time, but still mamma decided to go with him thinking the journey might do him good. But they reached Hartford he became very sick, and his trouble prooved to be diptheria. He died about a week after mamma and papa reached Hartford. Little Langdon was burried by the side of

Grandpa at Elmira N.Y. After that mamma became very very ill, so ill that there seemed great danger of death, but with a great deal of good care she recovered.

Some months afterward mamma and Papa went to Europe and stayed for a time in Scotland and England. In Scotland Mamma and Papa became very well equainted with Dr. John Brown the author of "Rab and His Friends" and he mett but was not so well equainted with Mr. Charles Kingsley, Mr. Henry M. Stanley, Sir Thomas Hardy (grandson of the Mr. Hardy to whom Nellson said "Kiss me Hardy" when dying on shipboard) Mr. Henry Irving, Robert Browning Sir Charles Dilke, Mr. Charles Reade Mr. Black, Lord Houghton (Muncton Milnes) Frank Buckland, Mr. Tom Hughes, Anthony Trollope, Tom Hood son of the poet and Mamma and papa were quite well equainted with Dr. Mc Donald and family, and papa met Harison Ainsworth.

Papa went to Europe to lecture and after staying in Scotland and England and making a flying tripp through Ireland, he returned home with mamma.

Last winter papa was away for many months reading with Mr. G. W. Cable, and while he was gone we composed the plan of surprising [him] when he came home by acting scenes from the "Prince and Pauper." It took us a great while to commit all that was necesary but at last we were almost ready and we expected [him] to come home the next day on which evening we had planned to surprise him. But we received a telegram from him stating that he would reach Hartford "to day at 2 o'clock." We were all dismayed for we were by no means prepared to receive him The library was strune with costumes which were to be tried on for the last time and we had planned a dress rehearsal over at Mr. Warners for that afternoon. But mamma gathered the things up as quickly as possble and hustled them into the mahogany room. Soon we heard the carriage roll over the pavement in front of the house and we all rushed to the doore. After we had partially gotten over surprise and delight at seeing papa we all went into the library. We all sat with papa a little while and then mamma dissapeared into the mahogany room. Clara and I sat with papa a while so as [to] prevent his being surprise of our seemingly uncalled for disertion of him. But soon we too had to withdraw to the mahogany room so as to help mama sew on bucles onto slippers and pack costumes into a clothes basket. Papa was left all alone; Exept that one of us every once in a while would slipp in and stay with him a little while. Any one but papa would have wondered at mammas unwonted absence, but papa is to absence minded, he very seldom notices things as accurately as other people do; although I do not believe in this instance he could have been wholely without suspicion. At last he went up to the billiard room and Jean went with him. Mamma as a special favor let Jean into this secret on condition that she would not breathe a whisper to any one on the subject especially to papa and Jean had promised. But when alone up in papa's room, it was very hard for her not to tell papa the whole thing. As it was she was undecided whether to tell him or not. She did go so far as to begin with "Its a secret papa" and then dropping varius other hints about the secret and she went so far that papa said afterwards that if he had beene any one else he should have guessed it in a minute.

At ½ past three o'clock we all started for Mr. Warners house there to have our rehearsal   Jean and the nurse went with us, so papa was left absolutely alone.

The next day the first information that papa got was that he was invited for the evening and he did not know that anything unusual was going to happen until sat before the curtain.

We got through the scenes quite successfully and had some delightful dancing afterwards. After we had danced for about half an hour Mamma seemed in quite a hurry to get home, so we put on our things and started for home.

When we entered the library a lady was sitting in one of the arm chairs. I did not recognise her and wondered why mamma did not introduce me to her but on drawing nearer to her chair I saw it was aunt Clara Spaulding! ****—

Mamma told aunt Clara that we would have the "Prince and Pauper" again in a few weeks so she could see it. So it was decided that we should have it again in a few weeks.

At length the time was sett and we were nearly prepared, when Frank Warner who took the "Miles Hendon" part caught a severe cold and could not play it, so papa said that he would take the part. Papa had only three days to learn the part in, but still we were all sure that he could do it. The scene that he acted in was the scene between Miles Hendon and the Prince, "The Prithee pour the water!" scene. I was the Prince and Papa and I rehearsed together 2 or 3 times a day for the three before the appointed evening. Papa acted his part beautifully and he added to the scene making it a good deal longer. He was inexpressibly funny, with his great slouch hat, and gait,! oh such a gait! Papa made the Miles Hendon scene a splendid success and every one was delighted with [the] scene and papa too. We had great great funn with our Prince and Pauper and I think we none of us shall forget how imensely funny papa [was] in it. He certainly could have been an actor as well as an author.

The other day we were all sitting, when papa told Clara and I that he would give us an Arithmetic example; he began if A byes a horse for $100— "200" Jean interupted; the expression of mingled surprise and submission on papa['s] face, as he turned to Jean and said "who is doing this example Jean?" was inexpressibly funny. Jean laughed and papa continued "If A byes a horse for $100— "200" Jean promptly interupted; papa looked perplexed, and mamma went into convulsions of laughter. It was plain to us all that papa would have to change his summ to $200; so he accordingly began. "If A byes a horse for $200 and B byes a mule for $140 and they join in copartnership and trade their chreatures for a piece of land $480, how long will it take a lame man to borrow a silk umbrella?"

Papa's great care now is "Sour Mash" (the cat) and he will come way down from his studdy on the hill to see how she is getting along.

A few months after the last Prince and Pauper we started for "The Farm. The farm is aunt Susies home and where we stay in the summers, it is situated on the top of a high hill overlooking the valley of Elmira. In the winter papa sent way to Kansas for a little donkey for us to have at the farm, and when we got to the farm we were delighted to find the donkey in good trimm and ready to have us ride her. But she has prooved to be very balky, and we have to make her go by walking in front of [her] with a handfull of crackers. Papa wrote a little poem about her which I have and will put in here, it is partly German and partly English.—

Kiditchin.

"O du lieb' Kiditchin,
Du bist ganz bewitchin."
　　"Waw — — — — — he!"

"Our summer days Kiditchin
Thou'rt dear from nose to britchin"
　　"Waw — — — — he!"

"No dought thoult get a switchin
When for mischief thour't itchin"
　　"Waw — — — — he!"

"But when youre good Kiditchin
You shall feast in James's kitchen"
　　"Wah — — — he!"

"Anon lift up thy song—
Thy noble note prolong,—
Thou living chinese gong!"
　　"Waw — — — he! waw — — — — he waw — he"
"Sweetest donkey man ever saw."—

Mark Twain.

Cats at Quarry Farm, 1887: Sour Mash, Apollinaris, Zoroaster, and Blatherskite.

There are eleven cats at the farm here now, and papa's favorite a little T. S. kitten he has named "Sour Mash" and a little spotted one "Famine."

It is very [   ] to see what papa calls the cat prosession it was formed in this way. Old Minnie cat headed, (the mother of all the cats) next to her came aunt Susie, then Clara on the donkey, accompanied by a pile of cats, then papa and Jean hand in hand and a pile of cats brought up the rear, Mamma and I made up the audience.—

Our varius occupations are as follows. Papa ris[es] about ½ past 7 in the morning, breakfasts at eight, writes plays tennis with Clara and me and tries to make the donkey go in the morning, does varius things in A M. and in the evening plays tennis with Clara and me and amuses Jean and the donkey.

Mamma rises about ¼ to eight, breakfasts at eight, teaches Jean German reading from 9–10, reads German with me from 10–11—Then she reads studdies or visits with aunt Susie for a while, and then she reads to Clara and I till lunch time things connected with English history for we hope to go to England next summer, while we sew. Then we have lunch. She studdies for about half an hour or visits with aunt Susie, then reads to us an hour or more, then studdies write reads and rests till supper time. After supper she sits out on the porch and works till eight o'clock, from eight o'clock till bedtime she plays whist with papa, and after she has retired she reads and studdies German for a while.

Clara and I do most every thing from practicing to donkey riding and playing tag. While Jeans time is spent in asking mamma what she can have to eat.— ✳✳✳✳✳✳✳

It is Jean's birth day to day. She is 5 yrs. old. Papa is away today and he telegraphed Jean that he wished her 65 happy returns.

Papa has just written something about General Grant's Getesburg speech. I will put it in here.

"General Grant."

Any one who has had the privilege of knowing General Grant personaly will recognize how justly General Beale recently out lined his great and simple and beautiful nature. Thirteen hundred years ago, as the legends of King Arthur's Round table have it, Sir Launcelot, the flower of cristian chivalry, the knight without a peer, lay dead in the castle of Joyous Gard. With a loving and longing heart, his brother the knight Sir Ector de Maris had been seeking him patiently for seven lagging years, and now he arived at this place at nightfall and heard the chanting of monks over the dead. In the quaint and charming English of nearly 4 hundred years ago the story says,—

"And when Sir Ector heard such noise and light in the quire of

Joyous Gard he alight, and put his horse from him, and came into the quire and there he saw men sing and weep. And all they knew Sir Ector but he knew not them. Then went Sir Bors unto Sir Ector and told him how there lay his brother Sir Launcelot dead: and then Sir Ector threw his shield sword, and helm, from him; and when he beheld Sir Launcelot's visage, he fell down in a swoon: and when he awaked it were hard for any tongue to tell the doleful complaints that he made for his brother."

Then follows his tribute,—a passage whose noble and simple eloquence had not its equal in English literature, until the Gettesburg speech took its lofty place beside it. The words drew a portrait 13 centuries ago; they draw its twin to day without the alteration of a syllable:—

"Ah Launcelot thou were head of all christian knights! And now I dare say, thou Sir Launcelot, there thou liest, that thou were never matched of earthly kni[gh]ts hands; and thou were the court[l]iest knight, that ever bare shield, and thou were the truest friend to thy [lover] that ever bestrode horse; and thou were the truest lover, of a sinful man, that ever loved woman, and thou were the kindest man that ever strake with sword; and thou were the goodliest person that ever came among press of knights; and thou were the meekest man and the gentlest that ever ate in hall among ladies, and thou were the sternest knight to thy mortal foe that ever put spear in rest."

S.L.C.

July *1885*.

The other day papa thought he would see how he could mannage Cadichon who had been acting badly so he got onto her but papa wanted to go one way and Cadichon another, and as papa wouldn't submit Cadichon threw him off into the high grass.

About a half an hour later Jean came down onto the porch in her nightgown and sat on Mammas lap. I said Jean what do you think!

Cadichon threw papa off into the high grass!" She answerd in a very calm way "I know it" I said how do you know it? she said oh I saw it from the window." She had been in the habit of standing at the window in her night gown and crittisizing the shotts papa and I made while playing tennis and we wondered why she did not critticize the way papa fell from Cadichon.

Papa has just written to the editor of [the] Sun what he thinks about Gen. Grant's burial. I will put it in here.

"General Grant's Burial."
Will the Captain be Removed?—
A Suggestion by Mark Twain.

To the editor of the "Sun."—"Sir: The newspaper atmosphere is charged with objections to New York as the sepulchre of General Grant, and the objectors are strenuous that Washington is the right place. They offer good reasons,—good temporary reasons,—for both of these positions.

But it seems to me that temporary reasons are not meet for the occation. We need to consider posterity rather than our own generation. We should select a grave which will not merely be in the right place now, but will still be in the right place five hundred years from now.

How does Washington promise as to that?—You only have to hit it in one place to kill it. Some day the West will be numerically strong enough to remove the seat of government; her past attemps are a fair warning that when that day comes she will do it. Then the city of Washington will lose it's consequence, and pass out of the public view, and the public talk. It is quite within the possibilities that a century hence people would wonder and say, "how does it come, that our predecessors buried their great dead in this deserted place?"

"But as long as American civilization lasts New York will last. I cannot but think she has beene well and wisely chosen as the guardian of a grave which is destined to become almost the most conspicuous in the worlds history. Twenty centuries from now New York will still be New York, still a vast city, and the most notable object in it will still be the tomb and monument of General Grant.

I observe that the common and strongest objection to New York is that she is not national ground. Let us give ourselves no uneasyness about that.

Wherever General Grants body lies that is national ground.

S. L. Clemens.

July 27th 85.

Papa says that if collera comes here he will take Sour Mash to the mountains.

The other day Jean was taking a walk with papa and as she passed the barn, she saw some little newly born baby ducks she turned to papa and said "I wonder why God gives us so much ducks as Patrick kills so many."

Papa has gone to New York to attend Gen. Grant's funeral. And he wrote mamma that the mourning put up for President Garfield was not to be compared with that put up for Gen. Grant. He wrote that there were a great many pictures of Gen. Grant just set in a sea of black.

Papa has come home to day and we were all delighted to see him. It was beautiful to hear him discribe the procession in New York in honor of Gen. Grant.

Papa's friend, Mr. Gherhardt a young american artist who made a bust of Gen. Grant has just received the privilege of making a statue of Gen. Grant. And we hope will get a part in the great New York statue.

"I wonder why God gives us so much ducks."
Illustration from Sunday Magazine, *24 May 1908.*

Aug. 24

Mamma and Papa have gone to visit Mrs. Wheeler the mother of the artist Miss Dora Wheeler, at Tannersville N.Y. and they will meet there Mr. and Mrs. F. R. Stockton, Mr. and Mrs. Dean Sage, and Mrs Mary Mapes Dodge. They are anticipating a delightful visit.

Aug. 29.

Mamma and papa have returned and they have had a delightful visit. Mr. Stockton was down in Virginia and could not reach Tannersville in time so they did not see him. And Mrs. Dodge was ill and couldn't go to Tannersville. But Mrs. General Custer was there and mamma said that she was a very attractive sweet appearing woman.

Sour Mash is a constant source of anxiety, care and pleasure to papa.

Mamma has given me a very pleasant little newspaper scrap about papa, to copy. I will put it in here.—

"I saw a rather disparaging paragraph the other day, that recalled an incident of the Grant obsequies. I was at the Fifth Avenue Hotel at night, when the large halls were crowded with a mob of American celebrites. As we were looking toward the great staircase I saw James Redpath throw a kiss to a man going up, who turned with a friendly smile and tossed back a similar salutation. "Who is that?" I asked "That—" said Mr. Redpath "is the man who made death easy for Gen. Grant." "Who—Shrady or Douglas? "No" said our friend "it is Mr. Clemens—Mark Twain. If it had not been for him Grant's death bed would have been haunted by the fear of poverty for his wife and children. "I wish he added I could tell all I know about Mark's noble and knightly generosity. But I do I learned only under the seal of confidence. Mark deliberately alows men who would have driven a hard bargain with Grant to malign him when he could crush them by a simple statement. But I tell you the time will come when, if the newspaper reports of this day are read people will ask why Mark Twain was not given the chief place in the procession. He did more than any living man to make Grant die without dread or regret. Mark is a better man than he is an author and there is no dought I guess that he is great with his pen." I recall this remark as I saw Mark sneeringly referred to the other day.

———————

Sep. 9th '85

Mamma is teaching Jean a little natural history and is making a little collection of insects for her. But Mamma does not allow Jean to kill any insects she only colects those insects that are found dead. Mamma has told us all perticularly Jean to bring her all the little dead insects that she finds. The other day as we were all sitting at supper Jean broke into the room and ran triumfantly up to Mamma and presented her with a plate full of dead flies. Mamma thanked Jean very enthusiastically although she with difficulty concealed her amusement. Just then Sour Mash entered the room and Jean believing her hungry asked Mamma for permission to give her the flies. Mamma laughingly consented and [the flies] almost immediately dissappeared.

Sep. 10th '85.

The other evening Clara and I brought down our new soap bubble water and we all blew soap bubles. Papa blew his soap bubles and filled them with smoke and as the light shone on them they took very beautiful opaline colors.

Papa would hold them and then let us catch them in our hand and they felt delightful to the touch the mixture of the smoke and water had a singularly pleasant effect.

"Papa blew his soap bubles and filled them with smoke."
Illustration from Sunday Magazine, *26 April 1908.*

Nov. 29th '85.

Papa was fifty years old last Nov. and among his numerous presents
The Critick sent him a delightful notice of his semicentenial; containing a
poem to him by Dr. Holms a paragraph from Mr. F. R. Stockton, one from
Mr. C. D. Warner, and one from Mr. J. C. Harris (Uncle Remus).

Papa was very much pleased and so were we all. I will put the poem and
paragraphs in here.

The Critic.

Mark Twain's Semi-Centennial.

MARK TWAIN will be half-a-hundred years old on Monday. Within the past half-century he has done more than any other man to lengthen the lives of his contemporaries by making them merrier, and it looks as if he were going to do even more good in this way within the next fifty years than in those just ended. We print below a few letters of condolence from writers whose pens, like his, have increased 'the stock of harmless pleasures,' and whom we have reminded of the approach of Mr. Clemens's first semi-centennial.

MY DEAR MR. CLEMENS:

In your first half-century you have made the world laugh more than any other man. May you repeat the whole performance and 'mark twain!' Yours very truly,

CHARLOTTESVILLE, VA. FRANK R. STOCKTON.

MY DEAR NEIGHBOR:

You may think it an easy thing to be fifty years old, but you will find it not so easy to stay there, and your next fifty years will slip away much faster than those just accomplished. After all, half a century is not much, and I wouldn't throw it up to you now, only for the chance of saying that few living men have crowded so much into that space as you, and few have done so much for the entertainment and good-fellowship of the world. And I am glad to see that you wear your years as lightly as your more abundant honors. Having successfully turned this corner, I hope that we shall continue to be near neighbors and grow young together. Ever your friend,

CHAS. DUDLEY WARNER.

To Mark Twain

(ON HIS FIFTIETH BIRTHDAY).

AH Clemens, when I saw thee last,—
　　We both of us were younger,—
How fondly mumbling o'er the past
　　Is Memory's toothless hunger!

So fifty years have fled, they say,
　　Since first you took to drinking,—
I mean in Nature's milky way,—
　　Of course no ill I'm thinking.

But while on life's uneven road
　　Your track you've been pursuing,
What fountains from your wit have flowed—
　　What drinks you have been brewing!

I know whence all your magic came,—
　　Your secret I've discovered,—
The source that fed your inward flame—
　　The dreams that round you hovered:

Before you learned to bite or munch
　　Still kicking in your cradle,
The Muses mixed a bowl of punch
　　And Hebe seized the ladle.

Dear babe, whose fiftieth year to-day
　　Your ripe half-century rounded,
Your books the precious draught betray
　　The laughing Nine compounded.

So mixed the sweet, the sharp, the strong,
　　Each finds its faults amended,

> The virtues that to each belong
> In happier union blended.
>
> And what the flavor can surpass
> Of sugar, spirit, lemons?
> So while one health fills every glass
> Mark Twain for Baby Clemens!

Nov. 23d, 1885.   OLIVER WENDELL HOLMES.

To the Editors of The Critic:

There must be some joke about this matter, or else fifty years are not as burdensome as they were in the days when men were narrow-minded and lacked humor—that is to say, when there was no Mark Twain to add salt to youth and to season old age. In those days a man at fifty was conceded to be old. If he had as many enemies as he had grandchildren it was thought that he had lived a successful life. Now Mark Twain has no grandchildren, and his enemies are only among those who do not know how to enjoy the humor that is inseparable from genuine human nature.

I saw Mr. Twain not so very long ago piloting a steamboat up and down the Mississippi River in front of New Orleans, and his hand was strong and his eye keen. Somewhat later I heard him discussing a tough German sentence with Little Jean—a discussion in which the toddling child probably had the best of it,—but his mind was clear, and he was bubbling over with good humor. I have seen him elsewhere and under other circumstances, but the fact that he was bordering on fifty years never occurred to me.

And yet I am glad that he is fifty years old. He has earned the right to grow old and mellow. He has put his youth in his books, and there it is perennial. His last book is better than his first, and there his youth is renewed and revived. I know that some of the professional critics will not agree with me, but there is not in our fictive literature a more wholesome book than 'Huckleberry Finn.' It is history, it is romance, it is life. Here we behold human character stripped of all tiresome details; we see people growing and living; we laugh at their humor, share their griefs; and, in the midst of it all, behold we are taught the lesson of honesty, justice and mercy.

But this is somewhat apart from my purpose; it was my desire simply to join THE CRITIC in honoring the fiftieth anniversary of an author who has had the genius to be original, and the courage to give a distinctively American flavor to everything he has ever written.

JOEL CHANDLER HARRIS.

Dec. 1884. Last winter when papa was away reading he wrote me a good many letters which I have kept and will put in here.

The first one is written in german.

Grand Rapids Mich.
Dec. 14 1884.

Mein liebes Töchterchen,

Wie geht es jetzt mit der Cleveland und der Buffalo Bill? Errinerst du dich an die Bergziegen, oder Bergschäfe die wir bei des austellung Buffalo Bills zu Elmira gesehen haben? Nun die arme Thiere sind neulich dur Schiffsbauch veloren. Diese unfall ist auf der Mississippi vorgekommen. Wer Dampfboot an einen versteckten Fels zerstört wurde, und obgleich Buffalo Bill und seine Indianer und andere Thieren gerettet ward, die Ziegen stürtzte sich gleich ins Wasser und man sah sie noch nie wieder. Auch ein oder vieleicht zwei von den Buffalonen ertunken wurden. Dass macht mirs Herz so schwer dass ich nicht mehr schreiben kann.

Schreib an mich wieder und noch wieder meine liebling

Papa.

P.S. Meine herzlichsten grüssen an deine Grossmama.*

Utika, Dec. 1884.

Susie, my dear, I have been intending to write you and Ben† for a long time, but have been too busy. Nach meinen vorlesung in Ithika ging ich in der Bier lager und fand ungefähr fierzig Stüdenten von Cornwell Universität dort gesammelt; und sie machten mich herzlich will[kommen] durch heftig jüchzend und klatchen in die Hände. Dann sangen sie viele prachtvolle Gesänge, mit Solo und donnerhaften Chor. Ich habe dort gebliebn bis nach mitternacht, dann machte ich ihnen eine hubsche Reden, und erzählte zwei kommische Geschiten, die waren mit grossen Beifal erhielt. Nach dem fuhr ich nach Hause und bald ins Bett gegangen wurde.‡

I love you sweetheart good-bye

Papa.

* [*Translation:* "My dear little daughter, how are Cleveland and Buffalo Bill now? Do you remember the mountain goats, or mountain sheep, we saw at Buffalo Bill's show in Elmira? The poor beasts were recently lost through shipwreck. This accident occurred on the Mississippi. The steamboat was wrecked on a hidden rock, and although Buffalo Bill and his Indians and the rest of the animals were rescued, the goats plunged straight into the water and were never seen again. Also, one or maybe two of the buffalo were drowned. That makes my heart so heavy that I can write no further. Write to me again and yet again my darling. P.S. My warmest greetings to your grandmamma."]

† [*Susy's footnote:*] When Jean was a little thing Clara and I taught her to call us Guck and Ben, and Papa thought "Ben" so appropriate a name for Clara, that he still calls her that.

‡ [*Translation:* "After my reading in Ithaca I went to the beer hall and found about forty students from Cornell University gathered there; and they made me heartily welcome with loud cheers and clapping of hands. Then they sang a lot of wonderful songs, with a solo and a thundering chorus. I stayed there until after midnight, then I made them a nice speech, and told two comic stories which were received with great applause. After that I drove home and was soon in bed."]

The following letter was written not long after "Huckleberry Finn" came out, it was an answer to a letter I wrote papa letting him [know] how much Margaret Warner (a friend of mine) and I had enjoyed reading the book together, and how much we admired it.

St Paul Jan 23/85

Susie dear,

I am glad you and Daisy had such a good time over Huck Finn. I wish I had another book like it ready for you.

Some young ladis school teachers—called on Mr. Cable and me yesterday afternoon, and they wanted to see my family and I showed them the picture and they were very complimentary about the group, but they said they thought Jean must be a rascal. So she is; Jean is a very attractive rascal and a very good rascal too.

The thermometer has been ridiculus for fully ten days now away down below zero all day and all night long. And this in a country where the only heating apparatus known is an air tight stove. Dreadful things they are. My windows yesterday comanded a principal street, but during the entire day I did not see a woman or a girl out of doors. Only men ventured out and very few of those. Yet at night the opera house was full of people come out partly to hear us and partly to get their noses frozen off I suppose.

I am very sorry to hear that Miss Corey and Miss Foote are sick. I hope you and Mamma and the rest of you will manage to make out with colds, and not go any further with that sort of thing. Your loving Papa.

Indianapolis Feb. 8/85

Susie dear

When I get home, you must take my Morte Arthur and read it   It is the quaintest and sweetest of all books. And is full of the absolute English of 400 years ago. For instance here is a paragraph which I will quot from memory.—And you too may learn it by heart for its worth it. There are only two other things in our language comparable to it for tender eloquence and simplicity, one is Mr. Lincolns Gettysburg speech, and the other has for the moment escaped my memory.

————The paragraph just referred to is given a little further back under heading "Gen Grant."

"There isnt that beautiful? In this book one finds out where Tennyson got the quaint and pretty phrases which he uses in The "Idyls of the king"—"Lightly" and "Ware" and the rest. Yes you must read it when I come sweetheart. Kiss Mamma for me; and Ben and Jean.

Papa

Chicago Feb. 3/85.

Sweetheart,

Mamma has sent me your composition, and I am very greatly pleased with it, and very much obliged to Mamma for sending it. I ment to return it to Mamma, but sealed my letter *previously.* So I'll get you to do it for me.

It appears that the violin is becoming quite the fashion among girls. One of Gen. Fair Childe's daughters plays that instrument I didn't see the girls exept the one that was a baby in Paris. They were away on a visit. It is said that one of them is very beautiful.

In this hotel, (the Grand Pacific) there is a colored youth who stands near the great dining room door, and takes the hats of the gentlemen as they pass into dinner and sets them away. The people come in shoals and sometimes he has his arms full of hats and is kept moving in a most lively way. Yet he remembers every hat, and when these people come crowding out, an hour, or an hour and a half later he hands to each gentlemen his hat and never makes any mistake. I have watched him to see how he did it but I couldn't see that he more than merely glanced at his man if he even did that much. I have tried a couple of times to make him believe he was giving me the wrong hat but it didn't persuade him in the least. He intimated that *I* might be in doubt, but that *he* <u>knew</u>.

Goodbye honey
Papa

Chicago Jan./85

Susie dear, your letter was a great pleasure to me. I am glad you like the new book; and your discription of its effect on Daisy is all that the most exacting and most praise-hungry author could desire. And by the way this reminds me to appoint you to write me two or three times a week in Mamma's place; and when you write she must *not* write. What I am after is to save *her*. She writes me when she aught to be resting herself after the heavy fatigues of the day. It is wrong. It must be stopped. You must stop it.

When it is your day to write and you have been prevented, see to it that the day passes without a letter, *she* must not write a line. Goodbye sweetheart

Papa.

Toronto Feb. 15/85

Susie dear, it was a good letter you wrote me, and so was Clara's   I dont think that either of you have ever written better ones.

I went toboganing yesterday and it was indescribeable fun. It was at a girls' College in the country. The whole College—51 girls, were at the lecture the night before, and I came down off the platform at the close, and went down the aisle and overtook them, and said I had come down to introduce myself, because I was a stranger, and didn't know any body and was pretty lonesome. And so we had a hand shake all around, and the lady principal said she would send a sleigh for us in the morning if we would come out to the College. I said we would do that with pleasure. So I went home and shaved.

For I didn't want to have to get up still earlier in order to do *that*; and next morning we drove out through the loveliest winter landscape that ever was. Brilliant sunshine, deep snow everywhere, with a shining crust on it—not flat but just a far reaching white ocean, laid in long smoothe swells like the sea when a calm is coming on after a storm, and every where near and far were island groves of forest trees. And farther and farther away was a receding panorama of hills and forests dimmed by a haze so soft and rich and dainty and spiritual, that it made all objects seem the unreal creatures of a dream, and the whole a vision of a poets paradise, a veiled hushed holy land of the immagination.

You shall see it some day

Ich küsse dich mein liebchen

Papa.

Feb. 6th '86.

We have just had our third "Prince and Pauper" and we have had more fun acting it than ever before, the programme was the same exept that Papa lengthened the "Lady Jane Grey scene" in which Clara was the Lady Jane Grey. He also added a little to the interview between the prince and pauper, by putting in a little scene behind the scenes to represent their talking while changing clothes. It was as follows.

Behind scenes.

Prince. Oh wait! I did not notice! thoust got *that* all *wrong*, that part goes behind. Wait, let me help thee <u>truss the points</u>. There now.

<u>Pauper</u>. Ah good your worship I did never truss a point In all my life before tis by the grace of God alone that my *rags* hang together.

<u>Prince</u>. Wait, again, wait! You see this goes this way, then this goes in here, then one turns this back so, and brings the other forward. There now it'll do.

<u>Pauper</u>. Ah good your worship, thou hast not disposed that rag to it's

just advantage, prithee let me give it the touch, that is familiar to it.

Prince. Ah thanks, thanks, here I dont quite understand how this relic,—ah good very good thanks, Oh wait the sword belongeth on thy other side, so thats right. Come.

(they go onto stage)

The addition to the Lady Jane Grey scene was this.—

(Pauper sitting despondently) (enter page)

<u>Page</u>. The lady Jane Grey

(Exit)

(enter lady Jane Grey bows low)

<u>Pauper</u>. Oh prithee let me, out!

Lady Jane. (surprised,—a little ruffled—with distant politeness) Let thee out! My lord since when must the prince of Wales sue to common Clay for leave, to leave his room when he would, you jest my lord! and I? I do not *like* it.

Pauper. (distressed) Oh dear lady *I* am not the prince of Wales!

Lady Jane. (still piqued and sarcastic) Indeed! perhaps thou art Ananias or Saphyra in sooth with practice your grace might serve for both my lord. (another toss)

Pauper. (distressed) Oh lady, *do* not be cruel!

<u>Lady Jane</u>. Cruel? I cruel! I left mine amusement to come and help thee with thy greeck.

Pauper. Greeck? Oh dear lady I know no Greeck.

Lady Jane. Aside. How strangely he acts. I grow afraid of him saith he knoweth no Greeck, and how strange it is that he should say that for its true! (suddenly and with terrified conviction) his mind's disordered

Clara as Lady Jane Grey and Daisy Warner as the pauper (in the prince's clothing), costumed for the Prince and the Pauper *play, 1886.*

Pauper. (stepping nearer appealingly) Oh gracious lady—

Lady Jane. (interupting and shooing off with her hand) Do not touch me! (here insert old scene given in book) Oh what aileth thee my lord?

Pauper. Oh be merciful thou, in sooth I am no lord, but only poor Tom Canty of Offal Court in the City prithee let me see the prince and he will of his grace restore me to my rags and let me hence unhurt Oh be thou merciful and save me!

Lady Jane. Oh my lord! On thy knees and to me!

(exit in a frightened way)

Feb. 7th 86. Jean who is just five years old, has learned the part of the lady Jane Grey by hearing us rehearse, and she can act it quite well making up for the words she cant get straight, by adding great emphasies to the ones she knows.

Feb. 7th.

I overheard papa telling Jean a story this morning, it amused me very much it was a story of such great variety, and indeed papa has practise in telling stories of variety as Jean is a child of variety and original ideas, and papa is too, (I mean such a man) so half of the story he devotes to his own fancy, (if Jean allows) the other half to Jeans; I heard only a part of the story this morning, so I asked Jean to tell it to me afterwards so she did, and here it is as she gives it.

"Well once there was a register who went out walking   He saw a school-house, and he went into the school-house; He saw the big children pushed away the little children in the cold part of the room. He went in a corner and warmed the little childern, and as soon as the little childern said it felt so warm, the big childern came and pushed them away   then the reg. closed and then one of the big boys said, he would put in his finger and try to open it and snapp closed the register tighter with his finger in. Then the little childern had the stove. Then the boy that was pinched, howled and cryed so, that the other big children couldn't stay in the school house. So they went out and looked to see where that heatness came from (they thought it came from the sun or from the ground) and they couldnt see. Then they went and borrowed quite a few baloons, and went up in the air, and they went up higher and higher and higher and higher and they let out a bird, the children were frosen when they put out a bird, the bird didn't know where he was, and he went among the clouds, and pretty soon he came back sailing back again and they sailed and sailed and sailed and went over oceans and seas and ships, and pretty soon they landed in Africa. Quite a few plain people and a few Indians came, and some lions and tigers, and the lions nibbled at the frozen childern, and couldn't bite them. Then a man came and said they were missionarys on the half shell and they must be thawed out. So they thawed them out, and pretty soon they got growed up to women and men, and were very good missionarys and converted many, and a[t] last wer eaten at a barbecue—.

Jean, who is very fond of animals, demands strictly animal stories from papa, for which I am very sorry, as I think his other stories are better. Here is another story, of papa's, told to me by Jean.

A Tiger in the Jungle.

Once there was a tiger lying in a jungle on a very hot day, he heard a cow in front of him "Moo,—"Moo" Moo" He got up and said he would have a real nice breakfast. But he couldn't catch the cow, and he heard a little calf, so he stopped trying to catch the cow and ran after the calf, pretty soon he heard a cat "Meau"—"Meau," still nearer him than the calf, so he chased the cat, then he heard a dog,—"Bow, wow," so he ran after the dog, then he heard a rooster "Cuck-adoodle-doo,"—then he ran after the rooster, round, and round, and round, the rooster seemed nearer, and nearer, but still he couldn't get it, at last he fell down dead, from tiredness. He had been running after his own tail.

This story was told in the same way as the two preceeding ones.

The Donkey what Could Talk.

Once there was a donkey and he went out walking. And he saw some children and he wondered why those children had books under their arms, And he thought he would go with them to see what they did. And he went into the school-house with them, and they showed him their books, But he couldn't understand the words in the books, so one evening moonshine, he thought he would go to the school-house, and eat some of the books. He went and ate, German books, and English books, and French books and all kinds of books, and had a great deal of stomach ache afterwards, And when the children came home they wondered where their books were, and they couldn't see where the books were, they couldnt see. Then the childrern said, "Why this donkey must have eaten our books. But the donkey said he hadn't touched books. Then the school-teacher came home and the childrern said that this donkey could talk. And the school-teacher wanted to hear him. So the childrern called him, and he came and spoke to them, and as soon as the people saw, and heard this wonderful donkey talk, they immediately asked him to belong to their church. So he did. And when the choir sang, he sang with it, but he was not satisfied to sing in company with others, fearing his voice, might not be distinctly enough heard. So he asked for permission to sing alone in place of the choir   his request was granted him, and he sang regulary after that, every Sunday. At last people got so much interested in him that he was ellected to be Member of Congress, which honor he also accepted; and he was the first donkey that ever was member of Congress. And finally he ran for President and so he was the learnedest donkey that ever was.—

Feb. 12. '86.

Mamma and I have both been very much troubled of late because papa, since he has been publishing Gen. Grant's book, has seemed to forget his own books and work entirely, and the other evening as papa and I were promonading up and down the library he told me that he didn't expect to write but one more book, and then he was ready to give up work altogether, die, or do anything, he said that he had written more than he had ever expected to, and the only book that he had been pertickularly anxious to write was one locked up in the safe down stairs, not yet published.

But this intended future of course will never do, and although papa usualy holds to his own opinions and intents with outsiders, when mamma realy desires anything and says that it must be, papa allways gives up his plans (at least so far) and does as she says (and she is usually right, if she dissagrees with [him] at all). It was because he knew his great tendency to being convinced by her, that he published without her knowledge that article in the "Christian Union" conscerning the government of children. So judging by the proofs of past years, I think that we will be able, to persuade papa to go back to work as before, and not leave off writing with the end of his next story. Mamma says that she sometimes feels, and I do too, that she would rather have papa depend on his writing for a living, than to have him think of giving it up.

Ever since papa and mamma were married, papa has written his books and then taken them to mamma in manuscript and she has expergated them. Papa read "Hucleberry Finn" to us in manuscript just before it came out, and then he would leave parts of it with mamma to expergate, while he went off up to the study to work, and sometimes Clara and I would be sitting with mamma while she was looking the manuscript over, and I remember so well, with what pangs of regret we used to see her turn down the leaves of the pages, which meant, that some delightfully dreadful part must be scratched out. And I remember one part pertickularly which was perfectly fascinating it was dreadful, that Clara and I used to delight in, had to [be] scratched out, and Oh with what dispair we saw mamma turn down the leaf on which it was, written, we thought the book would be almost ruind without it. But we gradually came to feel as mamma did.

Feb. 12. '86.

Papa has long wanted us to have an international copywright in this country, so two or three weeks ago, he went to Washington to see what he could do (to influence the government) in favor of one. Here is a discription of the hearing of the Senate that he attended.

Mark Twain in his Quarry Farm study, 1874.

Jan. 3o. '86.—

The Outlook for International Copyright.

WASHINGTON, January 3o.—It is the impression of those who
have followed the hearing in international copyright that the
Senate Committee on Patents will report favorably the bill with the
"printers' amendment," which is advocated by General Hawley, by
Senator Chase, by Mr. Clemens, and other publishers who are also
authors, and is accepted by the representative of the Typographical
Union, which, as the agent of that Union somewhat grandiloquently
told the Committee, through its affiliation with the Knights of
Labor, speaks for from 4,000,000 to 5,000,000 people. Although
it was clearly demonstrated to the Committee by Mr. Lowell and
others that the American author is the only laborer who is obliged
to compete with those who are not paid anything, the influence of
the book manufacturers, and of labor unions, and of the various
protected interests, is so strong in Congress that those who boast
that they are "practical legislators" will not support a bill solely on
the ground that, as Mr. Lowell put it, "it is a measure of morality
and justice." It is not, however, measures of morality and justice
that can control the most votes. Mr. Clemens, in his humorous way,
during the hearing said a very practical thing, in accordance with
which the Committee is very likely to act. He said that while the
American author has a great interest in American books, there are a
great many others who are interested in book-making in its various
forms, and the "other fellows" are the larger part. It is probable
that the strongest opposition which the bill will encounter in the
two houses will come from those who wish to maintain the present
system of "cheap and nasty" reprints on the ground that they wish
to make literature cheap. One of the interesting incidents of the
last hearing was the presentation of a memorial in facsimile of

American authors by Mr. R. R. Bowker, who used it to illustrate the fact that the American author is the only American workingman who has really to compete with unpaid labor. It is a curious pamphlet. It contains the autographs of the great body of American citizens "who earn their living in whole or in part by their pen, and who are put at disadvantage in their own country by the publication of foreign books without payment to the author, so that American books are undersold to the detriment of American literature."

Papa has written a new version of "There is a happy land" it is—

> "There is a happy land
> Far, far away,
> Where they have ham and eggs,
> Three times a day,
> Oh dont those boarders yell
> When they hear the dinner-bell,
> They give that land-lord rats
> Three times a day."

'86. Feb. 22.

Yesterday evening papa read to us the beginning of his new, book, in manuscript, and we enjoyed it very much, it was founded, on a New Englanders visit to England in the time of King Arthur and his round table.—

Feb. 27. Sunday.—

Clara's reputation as a baby was always a fine one, mine exactly the contrary. One often related story conscerning her braveness as a baby, and her own oppinion of this quality of hers is this. Clara and I often got slivers in ours hands and when mamma took them out with a much dreaded needle, Clara was always very brave, and I very cowardly. One day Clara got one of these slivers in her hand, a very bad one, and while mamma was taking it out, Clara stood perfectly still without even wincing; I saw how brave she was and turning to mamma said "Mamma isn't she a brave little thing! presently mamma had to give the little hand quite a dig with the needle and noticing how perfectly quiet Clara was about it she exclaimed, why Clara! you *are* a brave little thing! Clara responded "No bodys braver but God!"—

Feb. 27. '86.

Last summer while we were in Elmira an article came out in the "Christian Union" by name "What ought he to have done" treating of the government of children, or rather giving an account of a fathers battle with his little baby boy; by the mother of the child and put in the form of a question as to whether the father disciplined the child corectly or not, different people wrote their opinions of the fathers behavior, and told what they thought he should have done. Mamma had long known how to disciplin children, for in fact the bringing up of children had been one of her specialties for many years. She had a great many theories, but one of them was, that if a child was big enough to be nauty, it was big enough to be whipped and here we all agreed with her. I remember one morning when Dr. —— came up to the farm he had a long discussion with mamma, upon the following topic. Mamma gave *this,* as illustrative of one important rule for punishing a child. She said we will suppose the boy has thrown a handkerchief onto the floor, I tell him to pick it up, he refuses. I tell him again. he refuses. Then I say you must either pick up the handkerchief, or have a whipping. My theory is never to make a child have a whipping and pick up the handkerchief too. I say "If you do not pick it up, I must punish you." if he doesn't he gets the whipping, but I pick up the handkerchief, if he does he gets no punishment. I tell him to do a thing if he disobeys me he is punished for so doing, but not forced to obey me afterwards."

When Clara and I had been very nauty or were being very nauty, the nurse would go and call mamma and she would appear suddenly and look at us (she had a way of looking at us when she was displeased as if she could see right through us) till we were ready to sink through the floor from embarasment, and total absence of knowing what to say. This look was usually followed with "Clar" or "Susy what [do] you mean by this? do you want to come to the bath-room with me?" Then followed the climax for Clara and I both new only too well what going to the bath-room meant.

But mamma's first and foremost object was to make the child understand that he is being punnished for *his* sake, and because the mother so loves him that she cannot allow him to do wrong; also that it is as hard for her to punnish him, as for him to be punnished and even harder. Mamma never allowed herself to punnish us when she was angry with us she never struck us because she was enoyed at us and felt like striking us if we had been nauty and had enoyed her, so that she thought she felt or would show the least bit of temper toward us while punnishing us, she always postponed the punishment, until *she* was no more chafed by our behavior. She never humoured herself by striking or punishing us because or while she was the least bit enoyed with us.

Our very worst nautinesses were punished by being taken to the bath-room and being whipped by the paper cutter.* But after the whipping was over, mamma did not allow us to leave her until we were perfectly happy, and perfectly understood why we had been whipped. I never remember having felt the least bit bitterly toward mamma for punishing me, I always felt I had deserved my punishment, and was much happier for having received it. For after mamma had punished us and shown her displeasure, she showed no signs of further displeasure, but acted as if we had not displeased her in any way.—

But Mamma's oppinions and ideas upon the subject of bringing up children has always been more or less of a joke in our family, perticularly

* [Letter-opener, at this date usually made of bone or wood—*BG.*]

since Papa's article in the Christian Union," and I am sure Clara and I have related the history of our old family paper-cutter, our punishments and privations with rather more pride and triumph, because of mamma's way of rearing us, then any other sentiment.

When the article "What ought he to have done?" came out mamma read it, and was very much interested in it. And when papa heard that she had read it he went to work and secretly wrote his opinion of what the father ought to have done. He told aunt Susy Clar and I, about it but mamma was not to see it or hear any thing about it till it came out. He gave it to aunt Susy to read, and after Clara and I gone up to get ready for bed he brought it up for us to read. He told what he thought the father ought to have done by telling what mamma would have done. The article was a beautiful tribute to mamma and every word in it true; But still in writing about mamma he partly forgot that the article was going to be published I think, and expressed himself more fully than he would do the second time he wrote it; I think the article has done and will do a great deal of good, and I think it would have been perfect for the family and friends' enjoyment, but a little bit too private to have been published as it was. And Papa felt so too, because the very next day or a few days after, he went down to New York to see if he couldn't get it back before it was published but it was too [late] and he had to return wi[t]hout it. When the Christian Union reached the farm and papa's article in it all ready and waiting to be read to mamma papa hadn't the courage to show it to her (for he knew she wouldn't like it at all) at first, and he didn't but he might [have] let it go and never let her see it; but finally he gave his consent to her seeing it, and told Clara and I we could take it to her, which we did, with tardiness, and we all stood around mamma while she read it, all wondering what she would say and think about it.

She was too much surprised, (and pleased privately, too) [to] say much at first, but as we all expected publicly, (or rather when she remembered that this article was to be read by every one that took the Christian Union) she was rather shocked and a little displeased.

C. and I had great fun the night papa gave it to us to read and then hide, so mamma couldn't see it, for just as we were in the midst of reading it mamma appeared papa following anxiously and asked why we were not in bed? then a scuffle ensued for we told her it was a secret and tried to hide it; but [she] chased us wherever we went, till she thought it was time for us to go to bed, then she surendered and left us to tuck it under Clara's matress.

A little while after the article was published letters began to come in to papa crittisizing it, there were some very pleasant ones but a few very disagreble, one of these, the very worst, mamma got hold of and read, to papa's great regret, it was full of the most disagreble things, and so very enoying to papa that he for a time felt he must do something to show the author of it his great displeasure at being so insulted. But he finally decided not to, because he felt the man had some cause for feeling enoyed at [him], for papa had spoken of him, (he was the baby's father) rather slightingly in his Christian Union Article.

After all this, papa and mamma both wished I think they might never hear or be spoken to on the subject of the Christian Union article, and whenever any has spoken to me and told me "How much they did enjoy my father's article in the Christain Union" I almost laughed in their faces when I remembered what a great variety of oppinion had been expressed upon the subject of [the] Christian Union article of papa's.

The article was written in July or August and just the other day papa received quite a bright letter from a gentleman who has read the C.U. article and give his opinion of it in these words.—*

March. 14th '86

Mr. Laurence Barrette and Mr. and Mrs. Hutton were here a little while ago, and we had a very interesting visit from them. Papa said Mr. Barette never had acted so well before when he had seen him, as he did the first

* [It is missing—BG.]

night he was staying with us. And Mrs. —— said she never had seen an actor on the stage, whome she more wanted to speak with.

Papa has been very much interested of late, in the "Mind Cure" theory. And in fact so have we all. A young lady in town has worked wonders, by using the "Mind Cure" upon people; she is constantly busy now curing peoples deseases in this way.—And curing her own even, which to me seems the most remarkable of all.—

A little while past, papa was delighted, with the knowledge of what he thought the best way of curing a cold, which was by starving it. This starving did work beautifully, and freed him from a great many severe colds. Now he says it wasn't the starving that helped his colds, but the trust in the starving, the mind cure connected with the starving.

I shouldn't wonder if we finally became firm believers in Mind Cure. The next time papa has a cold, I haven't a doubt, he will send for "Miss Holden" the young lady who is doctoring in the "Mind Cure" theory, to cure him of it.

Mamma was over at Mrs. George Warners to lunch the other day, and Miss Holden was there too. Mamma asked if anything as natural as near sightedness could be cured she said oh yes just as well as other deseases.—

When mamma came home, she took me into her room, and told me that perhaps my near-sightedness could be cured by the "Mind Cure"; and that [she] was going to have me try the treatment anyway, there could be no harm in it, and there might be great good. If her plan succeeds there certainly will be a great deal in "Mind Cure" to my oppinion, for I am <u>very</u> near sighted, and so is mamma, and I never expected there could be any more cure for it, than for blindness, but now I dont know but what theres a cure for <u>that</u>.

March 14th '86.

Clara sprained her ankle, a little while ago, by running into a tree, when coasting, and while she [was] unable to walk with it she played solotair with cards a great deal. While Clara was sick and papa saw her play solotair so much, he got very much interested in the game, and finally began to play it himself a little, then Jean took it up, and at last <u>mamma</u>, even played it ocasionally; Jean's and papa's love for it rappidly increased, and now Jean brings the cards every night to the table and papa and mamma help her play, and before dinner is at an end, papa has gotten a seperate pack of cards, and is playing alone, with great interest, mamma and Clara next are made subject to the contagious solatair, and there are four solataireans at the table; while you hear nothing but, "Fill up the place" etc. It is dreadful! after supper Clara goes into the library, and gets a little red mahogany table, and placing it under the gasfixture seats herself and begins to play again, then papa follows with another table of the same discription, and they play solatair till bed-time.

We have just had our Prince and Pauper pictures taken; two groups and some little single ones. The groups (the Interview and Lady Jane Grey scene) were pretty good, the lady Jane Grey scene was perfect, just as pretty as it could be, the Interview was not so good; and two of the little single pictures very good indeed, but one was very bad. Yet on [the] whole we think they were a success.

Papa has done a great deal in his life I think, that is good, and very remarkable, but I think if he had, had the advantages with which he could have developed the gifts which he has made no use of in writing his books, or in any other way for other peoples pleasure and benefit outside of his own family and intimate friends, he could have done *more* than he has and a great deal more even. He is known to the public as a humorist, but he has much more in him that is earnest, than that is humorous. He has a keen sense of the ludricous, notices funny stories and incidents knows how to tell them, to improve upon them, and does not forget them. He has been through a great many of the funny adventures, related in "Tom Sayer" and in "Hucleberry Finn," *himself* and he lived among just such boys, and in just such villages all the days of his early life. "His Prince and Pauper" is his most orriginal, and best production; it shows the most of any of his books what kind of pictures are in his mind usually; not that the pictures of

England in the 16th century and the adventures of a little prince and pauper are the <u>kind</u> of things he mainly thinks about; but that, *that* book, and those pictures represent the train of thought and imagination he would be likely to be thinking of today, tomorrow, or next day, more nearly than those given in "Tom Sawyer" or Hucleberry Finn."

Papa can make exeedingly bright jokes, and he enjoys funny things, and when he is with people he jokes and laughs a great deal; but still he is more interested in earnest books and earnest subjects to talk upon, than in humorous ones. When we are all alone at home, nine times out of ten, he talks about some very earnest subject, (with an ocasional joke thrown in) and he a good deal more often talks upon such subjects than upon the other kind.

He is as much a Pholosopher than anything I think, I think he could have done a great deal in this way if he had studied while young, for he seems to enjoy reasoning out things, no matter what; in a great many such directions, he has greater abillity than in the gifts which have made him famous.

March. 21st. Sunday.—Here is another of papa's stories told to me by Jean.—

"The Generous Fender."—

———

Once there was a night.—and a pair of tongs and a shuvel came into the library, with the other tongs and shuvels, and puled out the anc-anifertent fender, from the fire-place, and began to kick it because they didn't like it, but the fender was good; but they went on kicking till the fender was full of dents, and spoiled. (The people of the house had gone out to a party and they staid away all night) So the tongs and shuvels kicked the poor fender till they were tired, and then put it back in its place.—

Here Jean stopped, she had forgotten the rest of the story, and I could in no way persuade her to go on.

March. 23 '86.

The other day was my birthday, and I had a little birthday party in the evening. and papa acted some very funny charades with Mr. Gherhardt, Mr. Jesse Grant (who had come up from New York and was spending the evening with us,)—and Mr. Frank Warner.—One of them was "on his knees" honys-sneeze.

There were a good many other funny ones, all, of which I dont remember.

Mr. Grant was very pleasant, and began playing the charades in the most delightful way.—

March. 26. Mamma and Papa have been in New York for two or three days, and Miss Corey has been staying with us. They are coming home today at two o'clock.

Papa has just begun to play chess, and he is very fond of it, so he has engaged to play with Mrs. Charles Warner every morning from 10 to 12, he came down to supper last night, full of this pleasant prospect, but evidently with something on his mind. Finally he said to Mamma in an appologetical tone, Susy Warner and I have a plan.—

"Well" mamma said "what now I [wonder]," Papa said that "Susy Warner" and he were going to name the chess men after some of the old bible heroes, and then play chess on Sunday.—

April 18ᵗʰ '86.

Mamma and papa Clara and Daisy have gone to New York to see the "Mikado." They are coming home tonight at half past seven.

The other day mamma got a new rug, and she wanted to hang it up in front of the dining-room door; (aunt Clara had come two or three days before) the rug was spread out by the door, and mamma was looking at it, and comparing it with the door, to see if it was broad enough, aunt Clara seemed to think it wasn't broad enough. Mamma said "Clara I've the greatest mind to lie down and see." "Lie down and see"? "why what do you mean Livy"? aunt Clara asked wondering. "Why I mean I've the greatest mind to lie down by the rug, and see how long it is; and then get up and measure by the door." "Well aunt Clara said laughing, it seems to me, that is the most orriginal way of measuring a rug, I have ever seen."

Last winter when Mr. Cable was lecturing with papa, he wrote this letter to him, just before he came to visit us.

> Everett House
> New York Jan. 21/84

Dear Uncle,

That's one nice thing about me, I never bother any one, to offer me a good thing twice. You dont ask me to stay over Sunday, but then you dont ask me to leave Saturday night, and knowing the nobility of your nature as I do—thank you, I'll stay till Monday morning.

> Your's and the dear familie's
> George W. Cable.—

April 19.

Yes the Mind Cure <u>does</u> seem to be working wonderfully, papa who has been using glasses now, for more than a year, has laid them off entirely. And my nearsightedness is realy getting better. It seems marvelous! When Jean has stomack ache, Clara and I have tried to divert her, by telling her to lie on her side and try Mind Cure. The novelty of it, has made her willing to try it, and then Clara and I would exclaim about how wonderful it was it was getting better! and she would think it realy was finally, and stop crying, to our delight.

The other day mamma went into the library, and found her lying on the sofa with her back toward the door. She said "why Jean what's the matter? dont you fell well? Jean said that she had a little stomack ache, and so thought she would lie down. Mamma said "why dont you try Mind Cure? "I am" Jean answered.

The other night papa read us a little article, which he had just written entitled "Luck," it was very good we thought.

The stories of prevailing interest, which Papa tells us is "Jim and the strainin rag" and "Whoop says I" Jim and the strainin rag is simply a discription of a little scene way out west; but he tells it in such a funny way, that it is captivating.

"Jim and the strainin Rag"

"Aunt Sal"!—aunt Sal! Jim's gone got the new strainin rag roun' his sore schin. A. S. You Jim, take that ar strainin rag off you sore schin, an' renc' it out, I aller's did dispise nastiness."

"Whoop Says I."

Good morning Mrs.   What is it yer got in yer basket? Fish says she. They stinc says I. Ter Hell says she. *Whoop!* says I.—

We all played a game of Croquet yesterday evening, and aunt Clara and I beat papa and Clara, to our perfect satisfaction.

"Mark Twain has reached his fiftieth birthday, and has been warmly congratulated on his "Jubilee" by most of the wits of his native land. As the Ettrick Shepherd said to Wordsworth, when first they met "Im'e glad you'r so young a man" So one might observe to Mark, and wish he were still younger. But his genious is still young, and perhaps never showed so well, with such strength and variety, such varacity and humor, as in his latest book "Hucleberry Finn." Persons of extreemly fine culture, may have no taste for Mark when he gets among pictures and holy places, Mark is all himself, and the most powerful and diverting writer I think of his American

Contemperaries. Here followeth, rather late, but heartily well meant, a tribute to Mark on his Jubilee:

"For Mark Twain"
"To brave Mark Twain, across the sea,
The years have brought his Jubilee.
    One hears it, half in pain,
That fifty years have passed and gone,
Since danced the merry star that shone
Above the babe Mark Twain."

How many, and many a weary day,
When sad enough were we, Marks way,
    (Unlike the Laureates Markes)
Has made us laugh until we cried,
And, sinking back exausted, sighed
Like Gargery Wot larx!

"We turn his pages and we see
The Mississippi flowing free;
    We turn again and grin
Oer all Tom Sayer did and planned
With him of the ensanguined hand,
    With Hucleberry Finn!

Spirit of Mirth, whose chime of bells,
Shakes on his cap, and sweetly swells
    Across the Atlantic main,
Grant that Mark's laughter never die,
That men through many a century
May chucle oer Mark Twain!

                By Andrew Lang.

Mr. W. D. Howells, and his daughter Pilla have been here, to visite us, and we have enjoyed them very much. They arived Saturday at half past two and staid till Sunday night. Sunday night at supper papa and Mr. Howells began to talk about the Jews. Mr. Howells said that in "Silas Lapham" he wrote a sentence about a Jew, that was perfectly true, and he meant no harm to the Jews in saying it, it was true, and he saw no reason why it should not be recognized as fact. But after the story came out in the Century, two or three Jews wrote him, saying in a very plaintive and meek, way, that they wished he wouldn't say that about them, he said that after he received these letters his consions pricked him very much for having said what he did—

At last one of these Jews wrote him asking him, to take that sentence out of the story when it came out in book form; Mr. Howells said he thought, the Jews were a persecuted race, and a race already down. So he decided to take out the sentence, when the story appeared in book form.

Papa said that a Mr. Wood an equaintance of his, new a rich Jew who read papa's books a great deal. One day this Jew said that papa was the only great humorist, who had ever written without poking some fun against a Jew. And that as the Jews were such a good subject for fun and funny ridicule, he had often wondered why in all his stories, not one said or had anything in it against the Jews. And he asked Mr. Wood, the next time he saw papa to ask him how this happened.

Mr. Wood soon did see papa and spoke to him, upon this subject. Papa at first did not know himself, why it was that he had never spoken unkindly of the Jews in any of his books; but after thinking awhile, he decided that, the Jews had always seemed to him, a race much to be respected; also they had suffered much, and had been greatly persecuted; so to ridicul or make fun of them, seemed to be like attacking a man that was already down. And of course that fact took away whatever there was funny in the ridicule of a Jew.

He said it seemed to him, the Jews ought to be respected very much, for two things pertickularly, one was that they never begged, that one never saw a Jew begging, another was that they always took care of their poor, that although one never heard of a Jewish orphans home, there must be such things, for the poor Jews seemed always well taken care of.

He said that once the ladies of a orphans home wrote him asking him if he would come to Chicago and lecture for the benefit of the orphans. So papa went, and read for their benefit. He said that they were the most forlorn looking little wretches ever seen.—He said the fact was they were starving to death. The ladies said they had done everything possible, but could not raise enough money; and they said that what they realy most needed was a bath tub. So they said that as their last resource they decided to write to him asking him to lecture, for them, to see if in that way they could not raise a little money.

And they said what was most humiliating about their lack of means was that right next door, there was [a] Jewish Orphan's home, which had everything that was needed to make it comfortable. They said that this home was also a work of charity, but that they never knew, of its begging for anything of any one outside a Jew. They said no one (hardly) knew, that it was a Jewish home, exept they who lived right next door, to it. And that very few knew there was such a building in the city.

May 6, '86.

Papa has contrived a new way for us to remember dates. We are to bring to breakfast every morning a date, without fail, and now they are to be dates from English historie. At the farm two summers ago he drove pegs into the ground all around the place representing each [king's reign] following each other according. Then we used to play games running between these different pegs till finally we knew when each king or queen reighned and in refference to the kings preceeding them.—

The other day, mamma went into the library and found papa sitting there reading a book, and roaring with laughter over it; she asked him what he was reading, he answered that he hadn't stopped to look at the title of the book," and went on reading; she glanced over his shoulder at the cover, and found it was one of his own books.

June 26./86

We are all of us on our way to Keokuk to see Grandma Clemens, who is very feeble and wants to see us. And pertickularly Jean who is her name sake. We are going by way of the lakes, as papa thought that would be the most comfortable way.

July 4. We have arived in Keokuk after a very pleasant

ABOUT THE TEXTS

The following notes describe the manuscripts on which these texts are based. They also briefly identify places and events mentioned in the texts. Names printed in Small Capitals direct the reader to an entry in the Biographical Directory.

Differing approaches have been taken in transcribing the works by Mark Twain, on the one hand, and those by Livy and Susy, on the other. Livy's and Susy's texts are allowed to retain more of the graphical conventions of manuscript—superscript characters, for example, which are lowered in Mark Twain's texts, as he would have expected. Mark Twain's double- and triple-underscoring have been rendered as small capitals and full capitals, respectively, as a contemporary printer would have done; in Susy's biography, we assume she was unaware of these printing-house conventions, and we render her double-scorings as such. In all these texts, editorial corrections are few: in Mark Twain's, because few are needed, and in Livy's and Susy's, because their errors are part of the texture of their distinctively nonprofessional writings. Text printed on a shaded background represents a newspaper or magazine clipping. Full-size [brackets] are the writer's own; subscript [brackets] enclose words or characters supplied by the editor. Footnotes in this book are "signed," in order to distinguish those by Mark Twain or Susy Clemens from those by the editor *("BG")*. The footnotes giving translations have been supplied by the editor.

The original manuscripts published here are owned by the following:

· Mark Twain Papers, The Bancroft Library, University of California, Berkeley: "A Family Sketch," "At the Farm," and "Quarry Farm Diary."

· Clifton Waller Barrett Library of American Literature, in the Albert and

Shirley Small Special Collections Library, University of Virginia, Charlottes-ville: "A True Story, Repeated Word for Word as I Heard It," "A Record of the Small Foolishnesses of Susie and 'Bay' Clemens (Infants)," and "Mark Twain by Susy Clemens."

~~

A Family Sketch
by Mark Twain
written 1896–97, 1901–2; revised 1906

Mark Twain began to write a memoir of Susy just after she died in August 1896. His project of commemorating his daughter eventually produced this sketch of the household at large, as described in the Introduction. The transcription renders the text as finally revised—with one exception. Probably well after the initial composition, Clemens made several substantial deletions, striking out whole paragraphs and pages while leaving them entirely legible. Because these deletions have an appearance of being "conditional," perhaps conditional upon the desire to shorten the text or to suppress personal information, these passages are included in our text.

Mark Twain mentions: "Rum, Romanism and Rebellion," for which see the Biographical Directory under James G. BLAINE; "the *Century* building," the editorial offices of the Century Company in Union Square, New York; "*St. Nicholas,*" one of the magazines published by that company; see the Biographical Directory entry for Mary Mapes DODGE.

A True Story, Repeated Word for Word as I Heard It
by Mark Twain
written 1874

The text published here has been prepared by comparing the manuscript with the first printing in the *Atlantic Monthly* (SLC 1874), and adopting only those *Atlantic* changes that are clearly necessary or that are likely to have been made by Mark Twain in the (lost) proofs. In dialect speech, the *Atlantic* used the apostrophe to signal every elided sound, or letter; the manuscript is far less

In Memory of Olivia ~~Susan Clemens~~
1872   1896   ~~704~~
              Early ~~Years.~~

A FAMILY SKETCH.   = Susy
                      ~~She~~ was born in Elmira,
~~[crossed out]~~   New York, in the house of her
grandmother Mrs. Olivia
Langdon, on the 19th of March, 1872. ~~over~~ ~~She was to wander
far in the earth; & by & by under that same roof where
her mother saw her first she would see her again — &
then not any more in this life.~~

She was a magazine of feelings, &
they were of all kinds, & of all shades of force;
& she was so volatile, as a little child, that sometimes the whole battery came into play in the short
compass of a day. She was full of life, full of
activity, full of fire, her hours were a procession
of enthusiasms, & each in its turn differing from
the others in origin, subject & aspect. Joy, sorrow,
anger, remorse, storm, sunshine, rain, darkness —
they were all there: they came in a moment, &
were gone as quickly. Her approval was passionate, her disapproval the same, & both were
~~[crossed out]~~
prompt. Her affections were strong, & toward some
— Especially was this her attitude toward her mother.
her love was of the nature of worship. In all
things she was intense; in her this characteristic
was not a mere glow, ~~radiating~~ dispensing warmth, but a
consuming fire.

The first page of the manuscript of "A Family Sketch."

fussy, reading, for example, *might a* (not the magazine's *might 'a'*), *mongst* (not *'mongst*), and *arnest* (not *'arnest*). Believing, after analyzing the evidence, that Mark Twain is responsible for few of the revisions evident in the *Atlantic,* we follow the manuscript's dialect closely. Little is gained by rendering it either "logical" or self-consistent; as Clemens wrote to *Atlantic* editor William Dean HOWELLS on 20 September 1874: "I amend dialect stuff by talking & talking & *talking* it till it sounds right—& I had difficulty with this negro talk because a negro sometimes (rarely) says 'goin'' & sometimes 'gwyne,' & they make just such discrepancies in other words—& when you come to reproduce them on paper they look as if the variation resulted from the writer's carelessness" (*L6,* 233). The *Atlantic* expanded '&' to 'an'' (instead of 'and') when it is Aunt Rachel who is speaking, and we have followed that practice. The first book printing (in SLC 1875) has been examined; it seems not to have received any further authorial revision.

A Record of the Small Foolishnesses
of Susie and "Bay" Clemens (Infants)
by Mark Twain
written 1876–85

This record of the children's sayings was written in a bound composition book with ruled pages. This record was kept by Mark Twain (and, in three entries, by Livy) starting in August 1876; the latest entry is dated June 1885. Some entries, written on versos, are clearly additions made out of sequence; if reproduced exactly where they stand, they would be chronologically out of place. They have been silently moved to their temporally correct locations. The text has been ordered according to Mark Twain's directions in the manuscript, and the directions themselves are not printed—e.g. "Skip the next 2 or 3 pages, for I wish to say a further biographical word or two about these children." This edition does not reproduce the author's memory-jogging notations of subjects he means to record; most were expanded in due course into full entries. The newspaper article "An Actor's Fatal Shot" is from the Hartford *Courant* of 1 December 1882; the obituary of Jacob H. Burrough is from the St. Louis, Missouri *Republican,* on or around 3 December 1883.

The ornaments separating the entries have been editorially supplied.

The epigraph—"And Mary treasured these sayings in her heart"—is an adaptation or recollection of Luke 2:19: "But Mary kept all these things, and pondered them in her heart." The "Modoc war" was fought in 1872–73 between United States troops and members of the Modoc tribe of Oregon and California. For Mark Twain's explanation of "the ombra," see page 33. "Vöglein" is German for "little bird."

At the Farm
by Mark Twain
written 1884

This supplement to "Small Foolishnesses" is transcribed from an almost-complete manuscript in Mark Twain's hand. Written between 1 June and 7 July 1884 at Quarry Farm, the manuscript consisted originally of eleven leaves; leaf 10 is missing. Leaf 11 became separated from the rest of the manuscript and has only recently been reunited with it. Despite the missing leaf, the text has no appearance of discontinuity, thanks to an added passage, written in shorthand by Mark Twain's stenographer Josephine S. Hobby, "completing" leaf 9, where his longhand text breaks off. The shorthand passage, rendered in natural language, concludes the anecdote in words that are clearly Mark Twain's; these words also appear in his *Autobiography*, where this text was partly quoted (*AutoMT2*, 223). The added passage was inscribed in 1906 when this manuscript was revised by Mark Twain. Two further authorial revisions in the manuscript, dating from that time, are not followed in the present text because they were made specifically as adaptations for the *Autobiography*.

Quarry Farm Diary
by Livy Clemens
written 1885

Livy's manuscript diary is written in a blank book with ruled pages. She made entries fairly frequently in the summer of 1885, and very intermittently thereafter, with the latest being written in June 1902. The text printed here consists of selections from the diary's 1885 entries; omitted text is signaled by bracketed ellipses. The title is editorially supplied.

Livy mentions: Cadichon, the donkey, named after the donkey in *Les Mémoires d'un âne* (1860) by Sophie, comtesse de Ségur; *Die Jungfrau von Orleans* (1801), Friedrich Schiller's tragedy about Joan of Arc; Arabella B. Buckley's *Life and Her Children* (1880), a popular biology text; *The Betrothed* (1825), novel by Sir Walter Scott; Thomas à Kempis, fifteenth-century German mystic, author of *The Imitation of Christ*.

Mark Twain by Susy Clemens
written 1885–86

Susy's biography of her father was written between March 1885 and July 1886, in a ruled composition-book. Mark Twain quoted and commented on substantial extracts from Susy's text in his *Autobiography,* parts of which saw publication in the *North American Review* in 1906–7 and in later editions. A transcription of the entire biography was published on the 100-year anniversary of Susy's beginning to write it (Neider 1985). All these versions printed Susy's text interspersed with the added comments and digressions of Mark Twain; the present edition is the first to publish Susy's work without the mediation of her father. The title is editorially supplied.

Transcribing Susy's juvenile writing presents an editor with some challenges. Transcription is done with reference to the writer's norm, and Susy's norm is elusive. There are many places where it is uncertain what character is intended, and whether it is intended as upper- or lower-case. Susy, her mind racing ahead of her hand, sometimes omits whole words, which we supply in [subscript brackets]. The word missed is usually obvious; if it is not, we offer the reader our best guess. Sometimes we avail ourselves of Mark Twain's own guesses, written into the manuscript years afterward. Outright corrections of the manuscript text have been kept to a bare minimum, but they do occur—on page 131, for example, where Susy distractedly wrote "flowers" instead of "flies."

Susy mentions (or the various texts she incorporates in her work mention): "mugwump," slang term for a Republican voter who withheld his vote

Concerning the government of children. So judging by the proofs of past years, I think that he will be able to persuade papa to go back to work as before, & not leave off writing with the end of his next story. Mamma says that she sometimes feels, & I do too, that she would rather have papa depend on his writing for a living than to have him think of giving it up.

Ever since papa & mamma were married papa had written his books & then taken them to mamma in manuscript, & she has expurgated them. Papa read "Huckleberry Finn" to us in manuscript just before it came out, & then he would leave parts of it with mamma to expurgate, while he went off up to the study to work. And sometimes Clara & I would be setting with mamma while she was looking the manuscript over, & I remember so well with what pangs of regret we used to see her turn down the leaves of the pages, which meant that some delightfully horrible dreadful part

Page 87 from the manuscript of "Mark Twain by Susy Clemens."

for the party's 1884 presidential candidate James G. Blaine; "the F.F.V.'s," or First Families of Virginia; "Gen. How," a mistake for "Gen. Hood" (Confederate general John Bell Hood, 1831–79); *Morte Darthur,* romance by Sir Thomas Malory (d. 1471); Alfred, Lord Tennyson (1809–92), and his Arthurian poem cycle *Idylls of the King;* two public readings by Mark Twain: "A Trying Situation," adapted from chapter 25 of *A Tramp Abroad* (SLC 1880), and the folk-tale "The Golden Arm," eventually collected in *How to Tell a Story and Other Essays* (SLC 1897); Ananias and Sapphira, proverbial liars (Acts 5:1–11); *The Mikado,* operetta by Gilbert and Sullivan, which in April 1886 was about to close its successful first American run in a production by the D'Oyly Carte Opera Company; *The Rise of Silas Lapham* (1885), novel by William Dean Howells. The German phrase on page 117 may be translated "Loving gift to Mamma"; that on 141, "I kiss you my darling." On page 124, "T. S." is Susy's abbreviation for "tortoise-shell." The word "anc-anifertent" (page 157) has not been satisfactorily explained.

In Andrew Lang's birthday tribute to Mark Twain (pages 160–61), "the Ettrick Shepherd" refers to James Hogg, the Scottish poet and novelist; "the Laureates Markes" alludes to a line in "The Last Tournament" by British poet laureate Alfred Tennyson: "'Mark's way,' said Mark, and clove him thro' the brain." Lang's "like Gargery Wot larx!"—not obvious in Susy's transcription!—alludes to Joe Gargery in Dickens's *Great Expectations* (1861) and to this character's repeated phrase "What larks!"

Detailed annotation to much of Susy's text—all of it that was quoted by Mark Twain in his own autobiography, which is most of it—may be found in the first two volumes of the Mark Twain Project edition (*AutoMT1; AutoMT2*).

ABOUT THE ILLUSTRATIONS

Unless otherwise noted, the images are from photographs in the Mark Twain Papers, The Bancroft Library, Berkeley.

Frontispiece: Mark Twain at desk. Photographer and date unknown.

Page 12: The Clemens family on the "ombra" of their Hartford house, 1884. From left to right: Clara, Samuel, Jean, Livy, and Susy. Photograph by Horace L. Bundy.

Page 17: The Clemenses' Hartford house. Photograph courtesy of the Mark Twain House and Museum.

Page 19: Photographs of the Clemenses' family servants Katy Leary and Patrick McAleer courtesy of the Mark Twain House and Museum; photograph of Rosina Hay, around 1874, from Livy's photograph album, courtesy of the Huntington Library, San Marino, California.

Page 41: Mark Twain's study at Quarry Farm. Photographer and exact date unknown.

Page 44: Mary Ann Cord. Leon Washington Condol Papers, Special Collections, University of Maryland Libraries.

Page 49: Henry Washington. Leon Washington Condol Papers, Special Collections, University of Maryland Libraries.

Page 52: From left to right: Clara, Jean, and Susy; Hartford, 28 March 1881. On the back of this print Mark Twain noted the date and the children's ages: Susy was nine years old, Clara six years and nine months, and Jean eight months. Photograph by Horace L. Bundy.

Page 56: Susy, 1873. Photograph by John Moffat, Edinburgh.

Page 59: Hearth in the library of the Hartford house, from "A Model State Capital" by George Parsons Lathrop, in *Harper's New Monthly Magazine,* October 1885. Engraved from a photograph by R. S. De Lamater.

Page 72: Illustration by William Page from his article "The Measure of a Man," in *Scribner's Monthly,* April 1879. Mark Twain's sketch from the "Small Foolishnesses" manuscript is reproduced courtesy of the Albert and Shirley Small Special Collections Library, University of Virginia, Charlottesville.

Page 89: Jean, 1884. Photograph by Horace L. Bundy.

Page 94: The Crane family home at Quarry Farm, 1903. Photograph by T. E. Marr.

Page 98: Livy in a railway carriage, July 1895. Photograph by James B. Pond. Courtesy of Kevin Mac Donnell.

Page 101: Clara and Jumbo, Hartford, 1884. Photograph by Horace L. Bundy.

Page 106: Susy, Hartford, 1884. Detail of a photograph by Horace L. Bundy.

Page 112: Langdon Clemens, Elmira, 1871. Photograph by John H. Whitley. Courtesy of the Mark Twain Archive, Center for Mark Twain Studies, Elmira College, New York.

Page 124: Cats at Quarry Farm, 1887. Their names, as given in the caption, come from Mark Twain's 2 April 1890 letter to Edwin Wildman, a magazine editor who had asked for further particulars of the cats. Photograph by Elisha M. Van Aken.

Page 129: Illustration by Emlen McConnell from "The Autobiography of Mark Twain," *Sunday Magazine,* 24 May 1908.

Page 132: Illustration by Emlen McConnell from "The Autobiography of Mark Twain," *Sunday Magazine,* 26 April 1908.

Page 143: Clara and Daisy Warner costumed for the *Prince and the Pauper* play, 1886. Photograph by Horace L. Bundy.

Page 148: Mark Twain in his Quarry Farm study, 1874. Photograph by Elisha M. Van Aken.

Page 167: First page of the manuscript of "A Family Sketch."

Page 171: This leaf of "Mark Twain by Susy Clemens" is reproduced courtesy of the Albert and Shirley Small Special Collections Library, University of Virginia, Charlottesville.

BIOGRAPHICAL DIRECTORY

AINSWORTH, William Harrison (1805–82). English author of historical novels.

ALDRICH, Thomas Bailey (1836–1907). Author; editor of the *Atlantic Monthly* (1881–90). A poet and a wit; Mark Twain said that "Aldrich has never had his peer for prompt and pithy and witty and humorous sayings" (*AutoMT1*, 229). He lived in Boston and in Ponkapog, Massachusetts, with his wife, Lilian (whom the Clemenses disliked), and their two children.

ATWATER, Dwight (1822–90). An employee of the LANGDON family business; in Mark Twain's words, "always useful in humble ways, always religious, and always ungrammatical" (*AutoMT1*, 374).

"BARONESS IN MUNICH, A." During the Clemenses' 1878–79 sojourn in Munich, they met a Baroness Freundenberg, "who" (Livy wrote) "has lost her property" (15 December 1878 to Mollie Clemens; Mark Twain Papers). She subsisted by taking in boarders and giving German lessons. Among her boarder-pupils were Clara SPAULDING and Mark Twain's nephew, Samuel E. Moffett.

BARRETT, Lawrence (1838–91). Prominent actor, famous in Shakespearean roles.

BEALE, Edward F. (1822–93). Union Civil War general. His eulogistic remarks about Ulysses S. GRANT were made for the Chicago *Tribune* in April 1885, as Grant lay dying.

BEECHER, Thomas K. (1824–1900). Minister. Half-brother of Henry Ward Beecher and Harriet Beecher STOWE. He lived in Elmira, where he was the controversial pastor of Park Congregational Church. A friend of Livy's family, he officiated at her marriage to Samuel Clemens in 1870; and he habitually wore a cap made for him by Susan CRANE.

BLAINE, James G. (1830–93). Republican candidate for President in 1884. Late in the campaign, a Blaine supporter, the Rev. Samuel D. Burchard, vilified the Democrats as the party of "Rum, Romanism and Rebellion." The resulting defection of indignant Catholic Republicans was believed to have swung the election for the Democratic candidate, Grover Cleveland.

BROOKS, Fidele A. (born 1837). A friend of Livy's family. Her husband was New York leather merchant Henry J. Brooks.

BROWN, John (1810–82). Scottish physician and popular author; the Clemenses had met him in Edinburgh in 1873.

BUEL, Clarence Clough (1850–1933). An assistant editor of the *Century Magazine*.

BUNCE, Edward M. (1841–98). Hartford friend of the Clemenses. After Bunce's death Mark Twain said he had been "in some particulars . . . nearer and dearer to the children than was any other person not of the blood" (2 December 1898 to Mrs. Edward M. Bunce; Mark Twain House and Museum, Hartford).

BURROUGH, Jacob H. (1827–83). A St. Louis boardinghouse acquaintance of Clemens's in the early 1850s, when Clemens was a journeyman printer and Burrough a journeyman chairmaker.

BURTON, Nathaniel J. (1824–87). Pastor of Hartford's Fourth Congregational Church and, later, of Park Congregational Church.

BUSHNELL, Horace (1802–76). Theologian; from 1833 to 1859, minister of Hartford's North Church of Christ (later Park Congregational Church).

CABLE, George Washington (1844–1925). Louisiana-born author, famous for stories of Creole life. In 1884–85, Cable and Mark Twain made a joint lecture tour. Cable, a strict Presbyterian, did not travel on Sundays (the point of his letter on page 159).

CAREY, William (1858–1901). An assistant editor of the *Century Magazine*.

CARNOT, Marie François Sadi (1837–94). Fourth president of the French Republic; assassinated at Lyons on 24 June 1894 by an Italian anarchist. At the time, the Clemenses (minus Clara, who was in Paris) were staying at La Bourboule-les-Bains, in central France, where anti-Italian rioting erupted.

"CHARLIE, COUSIN." See WEBSTER, Charles L.

"CHARLEY, UNCLE." See LANGDON, Charles J.

CLARKE, William Fayal (1855–1937). An editor at *St. Nicholas* magazine from its founding; see Mary Mapes DODGE.

CHENEY family. Hartford business executive Frank W. Cheney and his wife, Mary (the daughter of Horace BUSHNELL), had a large family, with whom the Clemenses were intimate.

CLEMENS, Jane Lampton (1803–90). Mark Twain's mother. Born in Kentucky, she married John Marshall Clemens (1798–1847). In Hannibal, Missouri, she raised four children to adulthood: Orion (1825–97), Pamela (1827–1904), Samuel (1835–1910), and Henry (1838–58); three others, Pleasant, Margaret, and Benjamin, died in childhood. From 1882 she lived with Orion and his wife in Keokuk, Iowa. Mark Twain paid tribute to her in his essay "Jane Lampton Clemens" (*Inds*, 82–92).

CLEMENS, Olivia ("Livy") (1845–1904). Born Olivia Louise Langdon in Elmira, New York, the daughter of Jervis LANGDON. Her health was always delicate. In 1867 she met Samuel Clemens, who was captivated, and courted her energetically. They married on 2 February 1870 and settled in Buffalo, New York. Their first child, Langdon, was born in November; he died of diphtheria in 1872. In 1871 they moved, as renters, to the Nook Farm neighborhood of Hartford, Connecticut, a literary and intellectual enclave where they quickly established themselves. There they built the distinctive house which was their home from 1874 to 1891. In Hartford, Livy raised three daughters, and oversaw a large household with many servants, guests, and visitors; summers were usually spent at Quarry Farm outside Elmira, the home of her sister Susan Crane. In June 1891, mounting expenses and bad investments forced the Clemenses to close the Hartford house; they moved to Europe. In 1895–96 Livy and daughter Clara accompanied Clemens on his around-the-world lecture tour. The death of their daughter Susy in 1896 was a blow from which she never recovered. She died of heart failure in Italy in June 1904.

CLEMENS, Susy (1872–96). Full name Olivia Susan Clemens. Called "Susy" ("Susie," in earlier years). Nicknames: "Megalopis." "The Modoc." Mark

Twain's eldest daughter. Born at the Langdon family home in Elmira, her education was conducted largely by her mother and governesses. Her talents for writing, dramatics, and music were early apparent. She began her biography of her father in March 1885, when she had just turned thirteen. In 1890 she enrolled at Bryn Mawr College, but completed only one semester. After the family moved to Europe, Susy suffered increasingly from physical and nervous complaints. She declined to go with her father, mother, and sister Clara on the around-the-world lecture tour (1895–96), instead staying with her sister Jean and their aunt Susan Crane in Elmira. In August 1896, while visiting Hartford, Susy succumbed to spinal meningitis. She died in the Hartford house while her mother and sister were crossing the Atlantic from England to be with her.

Clemens, Clara (1874–1962). Nicknames: "Bay." "Ben." Born at Quarry Farm, she was mostly educated at home by her mother and governesses. During the family's sojourn in Europe between 1891 and 1900, Clara enjoyed more independence than her sisters. The family settled in Vienna in 1897, partly so that Clara could study piano under Theodor Leschetizky. By 1898 Clara's vocation had changed from pianist to singer, a career in which she found more indulgence than acclaim. She married Russian pianist Ossip Gabrilowitsch in 1909; their daughter, Nina (1910–66), was Mark Twain's last direct descendant. Between 1904 and 1910 Clara lost her mother, her sister Jean, and her father; at the age of thirty-five, she was sole heir to her father's estate. Gabrilowitsch died in 1936; in 1944 Clara married Russian conductor Jacques Samossoud. Her memoir *My Father, Mark Twain* was published in 1931. Her final decades were passed in California.

Clemens, Jean (1880–1909). Full name Jane Lampton Clemens. Born at Quarry Farm, she was educated largely at home. At the age of sixteen she suffered her first epileptic seizure; over the next several years her anxious parents tried to forestall the progress of her illness with various spas and treatments. Her condition, and the household's frequent relocations, gave Jean little chance to develop an independent life. She loved horseback riding and other outdoor activities, and espoused animal and human rights causes. In 1906 Jean was sent to a sanatorium in Katonah, New York, which she felt to be "exile"; she was there, and under care elsewhere, until April 1909, when she was allowed to rejoin her father at his newly built house in Redding, Connecticut. Over the next months she enjoyed a close, happy relationship with him. Jean died on 24 December 1909, apparently of a heart attack suffered during a seizure.

COLT family. In the 1880s, the surviving family of Hartford arms manufacturer Samuel Colt (1814–62) were his widow, Elizabeth Jarvis Colt (1826–1905), and their adult son, Caldwell (1858–94). Mrs. Colt was the unofficial director of the business and a prominent philanthropist.

CORD, Mary Ann (1798–1888). Born a slave in Maryland. She, her husband and children were sold on the auction block at Richmond, Virginia, around 1852. One of her sons, Henry WASHINGTON, escaped slavery and settled in Elmira, where he brought his mother to live after the Civil War. She married a local man, Primus Cord, and became a cook in the household of Susan and Theodore CRANE. In the summer of 1874, she related her life's story to Mark Twain, who adapted it as "A True Story, Repeated Word for Word as I Heard It."

COREY, Susan (born 1866). Susy and Clara's tutor in the 1880s.

CRANE, Susan (1836–1924). Born Susan Dean, she was adopted by Livy's parents. She and her husband Theodore Crane lived at Quarry Farm, just outside of Elmira, New York. She was very close to all the Clemenses.

CUSTER, Elizabeth (1842–1933). Widow of General George A. Custer, who died at the battle of the Little Big Horn. She published three books memorializing her husband, the last of them (*Tenting on the Plains*, 1887) through Mark Twain's firm, Charles L. Webster and Company.

DEVENS, Charles, Jr. (1820–91). Union Civil War general. Commanded divisions at battles in Virginia including Fredericksburg, Cold Harbor, and Petersburg.

DODGE, Mary Mapes (1831–1905). Children's author (*Hans Brinker and the Silver Skates*, 1865) and friend of the Clemens family. Founding editor of *St. Nicholas: An Illustrated Magazine for Young Folks*. Published by the Century Company, it printed work by—among many others—Louisa May Alcott, Joel Chandler Harris, Charles Kingsley, Rudyard Kipling, Robert Louis Stevenson, and Mark Twain.

DUNHAM, Samuel G. (1849–1934). Business executive; member of a wealthy Hartford family. He often played billiards at Mark Twain's house. With his wife, Alice, he had six children.

"EGYPTIAN, THE." See MCLAUGHLIN, Maria.

ELISE (also "Elisa" and "Elize"). German-born nursemaid, in the family's service from 1883 to 1887.

"ENGLISH MARY." A name Clemens used to conceal the identity of Lizzie WILLS.

FAIRCHILD, Lucius (1831–96). Union Civil War general. After the war he was a three-term governor of Wisconsin, then held a variety of diplomatic posts. He was consul general at Paris when the Clemenses met him, his wife Frances, and their three daughters, in 1879.

FIELDS, James T. (1817–81). Head of the eminent publishing firm of Ticknor and Fields, in Boston (later Fields, Osgood and Co.).

FOOTE, Lilly Gillette (1860–1932). Susy and Clara's Hartford governess from about 1880.

FRANKLIN, William B. (1823–1903). Union Civil War general; afterwards manager of the Colt arms manufacturing company in Hartford.

GAY family. Julius Gay (1834–1918), banker and historian, and his wife, Maria, had four daughters; they lived in Farmington, Connecticut. Maria Gay was a close friend of Livy's.

GERHARDT, Karl (1853–1940). Hartford-based sculptor; with Mark Twain's help, studied art in Paris. On returning to the United States in 1884, Gerhardt received some important commissions; his career later faltered.

GILLETTE. The "Gillette place" referred to in "Small Foolishnesses" was the residence (from 1884) of George WARNER's family.

GLEASON, Rachel Brooks (1820–1905). Physician and pioneer in women's health. With her husband, Silas, she operated a health resort in the hills just outside Elmira. Rachel Brooks was Livy's physician, and delivered all three Clemens daughters.

GOODWIN, Francis (1839–1923). Hartford clergyman, wealthy businessman, and amateur architect.

GRANT, Ulysses S. (1822–85). Commanding general of the Union Army in the Civil War; later, eighteenth president of the United States. Mark Twain published his *Personal Memoirs* in 1885–86. Colonel Frederick D. Grant (1850–1912) was his eldest son; Jesse Root Grant (1858–1934), his youngest.

GRIFFIN, George (1849?–97). Born in Virginia, he was the Clemenses' butler from about 1875 until 1891, when they moved to Europe. The fullest records of his life are the documents published in this book.

HAMERSLEY, William (1838–1920). Attorney; state prosecutor for Hartford County from 1868 to 1888; later a judge.

HARRIS, Joel Chandler (1848–1908). Georgia-born author of the "Uncle Remus" stories.

HAY, Rosina (1852?–1926). German-born nursemaid and tutor, hired in 1874. Called "Rosa." In 1883 she married Horace Terwilliger and moved with him to Elmira.

HAWLEY, Joseph Roswell (1826–1905). Civil War general, Republican Party leader, co-owner of the Hartford *Courant,* Connecticut representative and senator and, briefly, governor. A Hartford neighbor of the Clemenses'.

HESSE, Fanny C. (1821?–1907). A friend of Susan WARNER's. Served as Mark Twain's personal secretary in 1876–77.

HILLYER, Drayton (1816–1908). Insurance tycoon; also president of the Hartford Engineering Company, in which Mark Twain made a large and unprofitable investment.

HOLMES, Oliver Wendell (1809–94). Physician, author, Harvard professor; in his time, considered one of America's foremost poets.

HOOKER, John (1816–1901). Among the original residents of the Nook Farm community in Hartford. His wife, Isabella Beecher Hooker (1822–1907), was a half-sister of Henry Ward Beecher and Harriet Beecher STOWE. The Clemenses' first home in Hartford was the Hooker house, which they rented (from October 1871 to September 1874) while building their own home nearby.

HOWELLS, William Dean (1837–1920). Prominent novelist, editor, and critic; close friend of Mark Twain. Editor (1871–81) of the *Atlantic Monthly.*

He lived in Cambridge, Massachusetts, with his wife, Elinor, and their children: Winifred, John, and Mildred (called "Pilla").

HUTTON, Laurence (1843–1904). Drama critic. He and his wife, Eleanor, lived in New York, and later in Princeton, New Jersey.

IRVING, Henry (1838–1905). Shakespearean actor and theatrical impresario.

JEWELL, Marshall (1825–83). Republican party politician, two-term governor of Connecticut, and United States minister to Russia. Hartford resident and friend of the Clemenses'.

JOHNSON, Robert Underwood (1853–1937). Associate editor of the *Century Magazine* and tireless literary politician. Mark Twain privately characterized him as "Robert Undershirt Johnson—The great American undertaker—He'll undertake anything that can add to his popularity" (Lyon 1907, entry for 11 March).

KINGSLEY, Charles (1819–75), prominent English clergyman, Cambridge history professor, novelist, and poet.

KIPLING, Rudyard (1865–1936). The Anglo-Indian writer was only twenty-four when he visited Mark Twain in Elmira in August, 1889. Kipling's subsequent rise to fame, as well as his writings, made a deep impression on the Clemenses.

LANG, Andrew (1844–1912). Prolific British folklorist, anthropologist, and historian; a warm admirer of Mark Twain's writings—with the exception of *Connecticut Yankee*.

LANGDON, Susie. See CRANE, Susan.

LANGDON, Jervis (1809–70). Livy's father. He married Olivia Lewis (1810–90) in 1832, and the pair settled in Elmira in 1845. He became wealthy in the coal trade. The Langdon household was strongly religious and ardently abolitionist. Besides Livy, the Langdons had a son, Charles J. LANGDON, and an adopted daughter, Susan CRANE.

LANGDON, Charles J. (1849–1916). Livy's brother. Succeeded to the Langdon family coal business. He lived with his wife and children in Elmira.

LEARY, Katy (1856–1934). Born to Irish immigrants in Elmira, she came to serve the Clemenses in Hartford in 1880, leaving only after Mark Twain's death in 1910. She later ran a boardinghouse in New York City. Her memoirs, "as told to" Mary Lawton, were published as *A Lifetime with Mark Twain* (Lawton 1925).

LEWIS, John T. (1835–1906). Born in Maryland, where he lived as a black freeman. He settled in Elmira in 1864, working for the Langdons as coachman. He then went into business as a blacksmith; still later, he was the Langdons' tenant farmer at Quarry Farm. His wife's name was Mary.

MACDONALD, George (1824–1905). Scottish novelist and children's author. The Clemenses met him and his wife, Louisa, when MacDonald's 1872 lecture tour took him to Elmira. MacDonald's *At the Back of the North Wind* (1871) was a favorite with Susy and Clara.

MCALEER, Patrick (1844?–1906). The Clemens family's coachman. Born in Ireland; emigrated to America at age sixteen. With his wife, Mary, he had nine children.

MCLAUGHLIN, Maria. Briefly but memorably Clara's wet-nurse. Two years after this service, pregnant and about to be expelled from a charity ward for smoking and drinking, she asked Mark Twain for a letter of reference. Called "the Egyptian" in "A Family Sketch."

MILLET, Francis D. (1846–1912). Painter and journalist. He painted Mark Twain's portrait in 1876, and became a close friend of the family. He died on the *Titanic*.

NASBY, Petroleum V. Pseudonym of David Ross Locke (1833–88), journalist. As the boorish "Nasby" he lent ironic support to reactionary political positions.

NYE, Emma (1846–70). A school-friend of Livy's. She died of typhoid fever while visiting the Clemenses at their house in Buffalo, New York.

"PAGE THE ARTIST." William Page (1811–85), American painter.

PARKER, Edwin Pond (1836–1920). Pastor of Hartford's Second Church of Christ and a friend of the Clemenses'.

PERKINS, Charles E. (1832–1917). Hartford attorney; nephew of Harriet Beecher Stowe and of Henry Ward Beecher. With his wife, Lucy, he had five children. Mark Twain consulted him frequently up to 1882.

Pond, James B. (Major) (1838–1903). Impresario. He managed Mark Twain's public readings in 1884–85 and 1895–96. His "friend" "Miss Jessie" (page 118) has not been identified, but Mark Twain found it necessary to delete the reference to her when he used this passage in his own autobiography. Pond had earned his rank in battle during the Civil War.

"Rachel, aunt." Fictionalized representation of Mary Ann Cord, in Mark Twain's "A True Story, Repeated Word for Word as I Heard It."

Redpath, James (1833–91). Founder of the Redpath Lyceum Bureau, a booking agency for lecturers. Mark Twain's tour manager from 1869 to 1872, and a personal friend. In 1885 Redpath acted as stenographer for Mark Twain's dictations on his experiences publishing Ulysses S. Grant's memoirs.

Robinson, Henry C. (1832–1900). Mayor of Hartford from 1872 to 1874. "Governor Robinson" in "A Family Sketch"; although Connecticut Republicans twice nominated him for the office, he was never governor.

Rosa. See Hay, Rosina.

Sage, Dean (1841–1902). Wealthy lumber merchant, bibliophile, and angler. Mark Twain's friend and occasional financial advisor. He lived in Albany with his wife, Sarah, and their five children.

Sheridan, Philip H. (1831–88). A leading Union general in the Civil War. Mark Twain's firm, Charles L. Webster and Company, published Sheridan's *Personal Memoirs* in 1888.

Shrady and Douglas. George F. Shrady and John H. Douglas were two of the doctors who attended Ulysses S. Grant in his final illness.

Smith family. Mark Twain's reference to "the Norman Smiths" (page 40) is perhaps a slip. Among the Clemenses' neighbors was Charles B. Smith (1811–1900), a son of manufacturer Normand Smith (d. 1860).

Smith, George Williamson (1840–1921). Clergyman; president of Trinity College in Hartford from 1883 to 1904.

Spaulding, Clara (1850–1935). A close friend of Livy's from childhood, Clara Spaulding lived in Elmira. She accompanied the Clemens family to Europe twice, in 1873 and in 1878–79. In 1886 she married lawyer and politician John B. Stanchfield. Her sister Alice was also a family friend.

STANLEY, Henry M. (1841–1904). African explorer, writer and lecturer; founder of the Congo Free State on behalf of King Leopold II of Belgium.

STEDMAN, Edmund Clarence (1833–1908). Banker and man of letters. "I only despise him, I don't dislike him," Mark Twain told his secretary (Lyon 1906, entry for 13 December).

STEPNIAK, Sergius. Pseudonym of Sergei Kravchinski (1851–95), Russian revolutionist. He called on Mark Twain when passing through Hartford in April 1891, and was warmly received.

STOCKTON, Frank R. (1834–1902). Popular short-story writer and novelist, known for his humorous and fantastic plots.

STOWE, Harriet Beecher (1811–96). Writer and political reformer; author of *Uncle Tom's Cabin* (1852). She and her husband, biblical scholar Calvin Stowe, were Nook Farm neighbors of the Clemenses'. She was the sister of Henry Ward Beecher and half-sister of Thomas K. BEECHER.

TAFT, Cincinnatus A. (1822–84). Hartford's leading physician, and the Clemens family doctor until his death.

TAYLOR, Bayard (1825–78). Poet, translator, and travel writer; also United States diplomat, with posts in Russia and Germany. The Clemenses made an Atlantic crossing in his company in 1878 on the SS *Holsatia.*

TRUMBULL, James Hammond (1821–97). Historian and philologist; an authority on Native American languages. A Hartford resident.

TWICHELL, Joseph H. (1838–1918). One of Mark Twain's closest friends. Pastor of Asylum Hill Congregational Church in Hartford, where the Clemenses rented a pew. He and his wife, Julia, had nine children.

WARING, George E. (Jr.) (1833–98). Union Civil War colonel, agriculturalist, sanitation engineer, and essayist. His story "Vix," a loving tribute to his mare, was published in the *Atlantic Monthly* in 1868.

WARNER, Charles Dudley (1829–1900). Nook Farm neighbor, writer, co-owner and co-editor of the Hartford *Courant,* and co-author with Mark Twain of *The Gilded Age* (1873). From 1884 he and his wife, Susan (1838–1921; "Cousin Susie"), lived on the property adjoining the Clemenses' in

Nook Farm. Before that date, the house was home to the George H. WARNER family.

WARNER, George H. (1833–1919). From 1873 he, his wife, Elisabeth "Lilly" Gillette Warner (1835–1915), and their children, Frank and Margaret ("Daisy"), lived in a house on the property adjoining the Clemenses' in Nook Farm. They moved in 1884 to the GILLETTE house.

WASHINGTON, Henry (1842–1927). Son of Mary Ann CORD, by her first marriage. Sold on the auction block around 1852, he later escaped slavery by the Underground Railroad. Taking the surname Washington, he settled in Elmira, where he married and raised a family. He worked as a barber, eventually having his own shop on Water Street.

WEBSTER, Charles L. (1851–91). Married Mark Twain's niece Annie Moffett in 1875. In the 1880s he was Mark Twain's business manager and partner in his publishing firm. Personality clashes and ill health led to his retirement in 1888, less than two years before his death.

WHEELER, Candace (1827–1923). Pioneering decorative artist. An associate of Louis Comfort Tiffany, she helped to decorate the Clemenses' Hartford house in 1881. Her daughter Dora (1856–1940) was an artist and portrait painter. The Clemenses met them through Dean SAGE.

WHITMORE, Franklin G. (1846–1926). A Hartford friend and Mark Twain's business agent in the 1880s and 1890s. His wife, Harriet, was a close friend of Livy's.

WILLS, Lizzie. British-born nursemaid, hired probably in 1874 and with the family until 1877. The circumstances of her dismissal inspired Mark Twain's short story "Wapping Alice" (SLC 1981).

WOOD, Charles Erskine Scott (1852–1944). Soldier, author, painter, lawyer, environmentalist, and social activist. When Mark Twain met him in 1881, he was adjutant at West Point.

WORKS CITED

AutoMT1. 2010. *Autobiography of Mark Twain, Volume 1.* Edited by Harriet Elinor Smith, Benjamin Griffin, Victor Fischer, Michael B. Frank, Sharon K. Goetz, and Leslie Diane Myrick. The Mark Twain Papers. Berkeley and Los Angeles: University of California Press, 2010.

AutoMT2. 2013. *Autobiography of Mark Twain, Volume 2.* Edited by Benjamin Griffin, Harriet Elinor Smith, Victor Fischer, Michael B. Frank, Sharon K. Goetz, and Leslie Diane Myrick. The Mark Twain Papers. Berkeley and Los Angeles: University of California Press.

Clemens, Clara. 1931. *My Father, Mark Twain.* New York: Harper and Brothers.

Courtney, Steve. 2011. *"The Loveliest Home That Ever Was": The Story of the Mark Twain House in Hartford.* With a Foreword by Hal Holbrook. Mineola, N.Y.: Dover Publications.

Harnsberger, Caroline Thomas.

1960. *Mark Twain: Family Man.* New York: The Citadel Press.

1982. *Mark Twain's Clara: or What Became of the Clemens Family.* Evanston, Ill.: Ward Schori.

Inds. 1989. *Huck Finn and Tom Sawyer among the Indians, and Other Unfinished Stories.* Foreword and notes by Dahlia Armon and Walter Blair. The Mark Twain Library. Berkeley and Los Angeles: University of California Press.

Jerome, Robert D., and Herbert A. Wisbey, Jr., eds. 2013. *Mark Twain in Elmira.* Second edition, with revisions and additions by Barbara E. Snedecor. Elmira, N.Y.: Elmira College Center for Mark Twain Studies.

Lawton, Mary. 1925. *A Lifetime with Mark Twain: The Memories of Katy Leary, for*

Thirty Years His Faithful and Devoted Servant. New York: Harcourt, Brace and Co.

L6. 2002. *Mark Twain's Letters, Volume 6: 1874–1875.* Edited by Michael B. Frank and Harriet Elinor Smith. The Mark Twain Papers. Berkeley and Los Angeles: University of California Press.

Lyon, Isabel V.

> 1906. Diary in *The Standard Daily Reminder: 1906.* Manuscript notebook in the Mark Twain Papers.

> 1907. Diary in *Date Book for 1907.* Manuscript notebook in the Mark Twain Papers.

MTB. 1912. *Mark Twain: A Biography.* By Albert Bigelow Paine. 3 vols. New York: Harper and Brothers.

Nagawara, Makoto. 1989. "'A True Story' and Its Manuscript: Mark Twain's Image of the American Black." *Poetica: An International Journal of Linguistic-Literary Studies* 29–30 (Spring): 143–56.

Neider, Charles, ed. 1985. *Papa: An Intimate Biography of Mark Twain.* Garden City, N.Y.: Doubleday.

Salsbury, Edith Colgate, ed. 1965. *Susy and Mark Twain: Family Dialogues.* New York: Harper and Row.

SLC (Samuel Langhorne Clemens).

> 1874. "A True Story, Repeated Word for Word as I Heard It." *Atlantic Monthly* 34 (November): 591–94.

> 1875. *Mark Twain's Sketches, New and Old.* Now First Published in Complete Form. Hartford: American Publishing Company.

> 1880. *A Tramp Abroad.* Hartford: American Publishing Company.

> 1897. *How to Tell a Story and Other Essays.* New York: Harper and Brothers.

> 1981. *Wapping Alice: Printed for the First Time, Together with Three Factual Letters to Olivia Clemens; Another Story, The McWilliamses and the Burglar Alarm; and Revelatory Portions of the Autobiographical Dictation of April 10, 1907.* Berkeley: The Friends of The Bancroft Library.

ACKNOWLEDGMENTS

"A Family Sketch" was already planned to lead off this book, and its text was being prepared, when The Bancroft Library was able to acquire the manuscript at auction in 2010. I thank the Bancroft's director Elaine C. Tennant, and deputy director Peter E. Hanff, for all their support of the Mark Twain Papers and Project. Within the Project, I wish to thank general editor Robert H. Hirst for his guidance and encouragement. Project editors Michael B. Frank, Victor Fischer, Harriet Elinor Smith, Amanda Gagel, and Christopher Ohge have earned and double-earned my gratitude: over the several years this book has been in preparation, they have given unstintingly of their labor, expertise, and good humor.

In making this book a reality I have, not for the first time, profited from the incomparable attentions of the University of California Press, from whose number I must single out sponsoring editor Mary C. Francis and project editor Kathleen MacDougall.

At the University of Virginia, Charlottesville, which is home to the manuscripts of three works published here, it is a pleasure to acknowledge the cooperation of Nicole Bouché, director of the Albert and Shirley Small Special Collections Library. At Elmira College, warm thanks to Barbara Snedecor, of the Center for Mark Twain Studies; and at Hartford's Mark Twain House and Museum, to Cindy Lovell, Patti Philippon, and Steve Courtney. Elsewhere, I give thanks to Rebecca Carroll, Shelley Fisher Fishkin, Kevin Mac Donnell, Sharon McCoy, Linda A. Morris, Elizabeth A. Novara, and Barbara Schmidt.

∽ Acknowledgments ∽

Any errors or infelicities in the translation of German passages are due to my misunderstanding of the wonderful assistance given me by Holger Kersten, who is also the identifier of the Clemenses' "Baroness in Munich."

My part in this book is dedicated to the memory of my mother, Margot Griffin Kenney (1938–2012).

B.G.